TARTAN
THE HIGHLAND HABIT

HUGH CHEAPE

N·M·S

NATIONAL MUSEUMS OF SCOTLAND

This page: Near Banchory, Deeside. The autumn colours of rowan, bracken and birch are echoed by dominant shades in tartan.
Donald Addison

Front cover (inset): Piper to the Laird of Grant, painted by Richard Waitt in 1714. *NMS*

Front cover (background): Early nineteenth-century hard tartan in the sett that later came to be firmly established as Stewart of Appin. *NMS*

Title page: Lord Mungo Murray by John Michael Wright, about 1685. *SNPG*

Inside front and back covers: An early tartan worn by Sir John Hynde Cotton, 1744. *NMS*

First published 1991 by the National Museums of Scotland, Chambers Street, Edinburgh EH1 1JF

Second edition 1995.

Photography: Ian Larner, Joyce Smith,
 Doreen Doig
Picture research: Hugh Cheape,
 Alison Cromarty, Allan Carswell,
 Patricia Macdonald
Produced by the Publications Office of the National Museums of Scotland:
 Editor: Jenni Calder
 Series design: Patricia Macdonald
  assisted by Alison Cromarty
Typeset in Baskerville Book
by Artwork Associates, Edinburgh.
Printed by Clifford Press Ltd, Coventry.

ISBN 0 948636 70 X

AN ENDURING SYMBOL

When the Apollo spacecraft landed on the moon Allan Bean, one of the crew, reverentially laid a swatch of MacBean tartan on the moon's surface. Tartan is a symbol of kinship and belonging in Scotland, and a badge of identity recognized all over the world. Allan Bean's gesture was understood and applauded.

Alongside the powerful historical and national resonance tartan has for Scots is the fact that it has been borrowed repeatedly by fashion. Today, we are as likely to meet tartan in a couturier dress as in a kilt or plaid. Tartan is distinctive in colour, style and design. It conveys personality, ceremony and drama. All these aspects of its character have contributed to tartan being one of the best-known and best-loved fabrics in the world.

The origins of tartan are remote. Tartan's history is nevertheless fascinating, though it has been scrutinized with the eye of sentiment more often than of reason. Much of Scottish history has been dogged by speculation based on slender knowledge, by the mixing of truths and half-truths, and tartan is no exception. Its history has been coloured by strongly-held opinions and enthusiastic intuition, yet there is a well-documented story to be told.

The word 'tartan', probably French (from the word *tiretaine*), was in use early in the sixteenth century, a period when Scotland was dynastically linked to France. The French *tiretaine* described a half wool, half linen cloth, sometimes described in English as 'linsey-woolsey'. It seems likely that, in some way we can't now trace, this word came to describe the fabric we now call tartan.

The use of checks and stripes in patterning cloth was known in prehistory, and must be almost as ancient as weaving itself. A piece of third-century fabric excavated in Falkirk shows a simple check, a form of design which has survived, known more recently as 'Shepherd's Plaid'. Simple decorative weaving was known in all early cultures. Dark and light natural shades of wool were separated out and woven together in regular patterns. This early introduction of pattern into weaving shows how fabric and clothes were seen not just as protection but as an expression of creativity. That creativity has evolved a distinctive woollen cloth woven in a regular banded pattern, the fabric now called tartan – attractive, unmistakable and indissolubly Scottish.

An excavated fragment from Falkirk of woven cloth of the third century AD. Known as the 'Falkirk Tartan', the fabric uses two shades of natural wool in its yarn to produce a contrast. *NMS*

Reproduction of the twill weave of the Falkirk Tartan showing how the check of two colours and an intermediate shade is created. *NMS*

Above: Orkney sheep painted by William Shiels RSA, about 1835. These delicate little beasts with soft fine fleeces in a variety of colours were the survivors of the prehistoric domestic sheep of Europe. When clipped or plucked, the wool could be separated and spun into different coloured yarns to weave into checks and tartan.   *NMS*

Opposite: Tartan plaids woven in the nineteenth century in small checks of blacks and browns on a light ground. The use of undyed wool was common in weaving in both the Highlands and the Lowlands, although in the nineteenth century the 'maud' or 'Shepherd's Plaid' came to be regarded as a clanless Lowland check. *NMS*

Left: Shepherd's Plaid worn by a shepherd in Perthshire, about 1900. The plaid here became a traditional wrap, worn especially on the hills in winter and used to cradle lambs as well as to turn the worst of the weather.   *SEA*

TARTAN AND CLANSHIP

Tartan is made up from different coloured yarns woven usually in a plain twill to produce a multi-coloured check of colours and blends. The arrangement of stripes of coloured threads are the same in the warp (running lengthwise) as in the weft (running across), and the chosen colours are assembled into sets of varying thread counts. Each section of the design mirrors the section next to it. The resulting pattern is called a 'sett', and is now classified generally by the name of a family or clan.

Tartan was not originally an expression of identity. In the Highlands there were other emblems that served this purpose, for example sprigs of plants, shrubs and trees. But through the efforts of writers and artists, manufacturers and tailors, tartan developed over little more than a century as the badge of the Scottish clans. In the process, great significance and antiquity were claimed for many tartans, although in most cases the foundation for such claims was dubious.

Only Scotland appears to have developed the systematic weaving of tartan with this degree of sophistication. The adoption of certain patterns by clans and families has become a feature of the social system of clanship, and tartan is now a part of the definition of the Scottish clan. This describes the grouping of individuals or families who adhered to a local chief through kinship, feudal dependence, or some other reason – often security in the occupation of land. Traditional land rights were very important in Highland society, and held great emotional force.

Tartan has become inseparable from the kilt and plaid of Highland dress. In other parts of Europe traditional checked patterns declined and disappeared, but in Scotland tartan survived strongly, just as the bagpipes, also European, flourished. Due to geographical and cultural circumstances Scots were able to develop and enhance tartan, and its remarkable individuality ensured its survival in spite of adverse political and economic pressures.

For the descendants of Highland families now dispersed all over the world the old style of kinship is no longer tangible, but the need for identity survives. This readily focuses on tartan as the symbol of the old relationship, through a

Opposite: Selection of eighteenth-century tartans, woven with finely combed wool and tightly spun yarn. They compare well with surviving early portraits showing Highland dress. They cannot be classified as 'clan' tartans, as they were chosen for colour, design and flamboyance rather than identity. Most early designs such as these have since been given clan names retrospectively. *NMS*

simple equation of tartan and surname. Unfortunately, surname is never an accurate indication of either a common ancestor or blood relationship.

Clan identity has been fostered by clan societies, which began to be founded in the 1880s. The fact that they are still flourishing today is a reflection of the need for roots and a sense of belonging. A link with ancestry, tradition and history still conveys a strong emotional message.

Tartan has been adopted as the national dress of all Scots, Lowland and Highland, providing a powerful form of national, cultural and personal identity. Whether traditional or a recent creation, whether a symbol of nationality or a substitute for nationhood, tartan is no mean achievement.

Line-up of dancers for prizegiving at the Cowal Highland Games, Dunoon. The style of dress is specified in the rules of dancing competitions, and the preference is for 'dress tartans' with the broad bands of colour turned to white. Colour and display are the order of the day.　*Scottish Tourist Board*

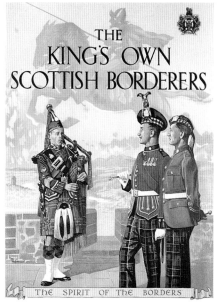

Recruiting poster by the Edinburgh artist Tom Curr for the Kings Own Scottish Borderers, a Lowland Regiment, demonstrating the force of the tartan-clad Highland soldier as a symbol of national identity.   *NMS*

The Pipe Band of British Gas Scotland, formed in 1986 and wearing the new William Murdoch tartan created for it. The tartan, based on the corporate colours of British Gas, was designed on computer in the Scottish College of Textiles, Galashiels, and named after William Murdoch (1754-1839), the pioneer of gas.   *British Gas Scotland*

C.H.S. del.t

Aquatinted by R. Havel

EARLY HISTORY

Early commentators were inclined to use words such as 'barbarous' to describe the Highlands and Highlanders, often with little direct knowledge of the people or their culture. Later historians were also often dismissive and inaccurate in their characterization of the Gael, noticing him only when he disturbed the peace.

Under the Lordship of the Isles there was a cohesive Gaelic entity, and culture and learning flourished. But the Lordship was dismantled in 1494, and there followed a period of warfare and power struggle, known to tradition as *Linn nan Creach*, the 'Age of Forays'. The attitude of many was summed up by James VI in his *Basilikon Doron*, the manual of kingship written for his son.

Opposite: This eighteenth-century vision of the dress of Celtic peoples shows a robed bard with clarsach and a figure in shirt and cloak. The saffron shirt or *leine*, possibly of linen, is worn under a brightly coloured, fringed mantle or brat. The artist-historian is extending back into prehistory elements of dress that were known from the later medieval period. The earlier mantle was a shaped garment, compared with the simpler plaid. Illustrated in Samuel Rush Meyrick and Charles Hamilton Smith, *The Costume of the Original Inhabitants of the British Islands*, London 1815.   *NMS*

Left: This sculpted panel on the tomb of Alexander MacLeod in St Clement's Church, Rodel, Harris, about 1528 shows the dress and arming for the chase and for battle without any of the later elements of traditional Highland dress. The figure on the left is wearing a saffron shirt, bonnet and trews. The figure next to him has a woollen jacket with loose-fitting sleeves over a quilted linen coat, and on the right is a figure in a mail coat over the quilted linen coat and pointed helmet of a Gaelic chieftain.
Royal Commission on the Ancient and Historical Monuments of Scotland

As for the Highlands, I shortly comprehend them all in two sorts of people: the one that dwelleth in our mainland, that are barbarous for the most part, and yet mixed with some show of civility: the other, that dwelleth in the isles, and are utterly barbarians, without any sort or show of civility.

There were attempts to draw the Highlands more firmly within the centralizing sphere of Scottish affairs, both by force and through political, religious and educational sanctions. The Gaelic language and Gaelic culture were threatened. The effect of this was, if anything, to reinforce a strong sense of identity.

Thirteenth-century Castle Tioram in Moidart represents one of the eastern outposts of the territories of Clanranald, a point of entry and departure in the 'Rough Bounds' of the Lordship of the Isles. *Patricia Macdonald*

The West Highlands and Hebrides were united to western Europe by the natural highway of the sea. Neither their situation nor their attitudes were remote and the Gaels moved easily between Scotland and the Continent for education, trade and military service. A reminder of this participation in western culture is the group of ecclesiastical buildings, including two churches dedicated to

St Mary and St Columba, poised on the edge of the Atlantic at Howmore in South Uist. *NMS*

Before the sixteenth century there is no evidence in Scotland for tartan as we would recognize it today. It is probable that checked and striped fabric was woven in natural and vegetable-dyed wools. Shades of red were favoured, and may have denoted status. The dress of the Highland man consisted of a shirt and a plaid or mantle worn over it, with the legs bare. But it is only in the sixteenth century that evidence for tartan itself becomes plentiful, though it is not specific enough to identify patterns or setts. In fact, the word 'tartan' has a number of meanings, referring to checked or coloured cloth, or to the type of fabric. By about 1600 it is evident that 'tartan' describes a woollen cloth woven in stripes of colour. It was not until the late seventeenth or even early eighteenth century that any uniformity was adopted by family, clan or district.

The evolution of the plaid was the key factor in Highland dress. It was simple to make, versatile, and classless – it was worn by the lowest and the highest. Tartan as we now know it owes as much to late medieval Highland dress as to technical developments in dyeing, spinning and weaving.

Samples of wool coloured with the dye of native plants: 1. Lichen. 2. Flowers of Goat's Beard. 3. Flowers of Ragwort. 4. Ragwort plant. 5. Bracken stem and fronds. 6. Heather. 7 & 8. Onion skins. The exceptions are the blue and green yarns, 9 & 10, dyed with indigo which became available through foreign trade in the late middle ages. Because this was a difficult colour to obtain, it was more exclusive and consequently admired. As George Buchanan wrote in 1581: 'They delight in striped garments and their favourite colours are blue and purple.'
NMS

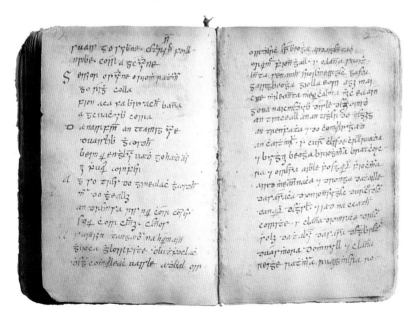

Pages from the *Book of Clanranald*, seventeenth-century manuscript in Hiberno-Latin script recording in classical Gaelic praise poetry the heroic virtues of the chieftains and leaders of society.   *NMS*

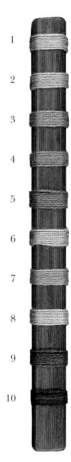

Carving on a powder horn showing a hunter and gillie coursing deer through an undergrowth of interlaced foliage and initials. The hunter is wearing bonnet, doublet, plaid and trews, the fashionable costume for men of rank in the late seventeenth century.   *NMS*

Lord Mungo Murray (1668-1700), a younger son of the Marquis of Atholl, painted by John Michael Wright in the mid-1680s. He is dressed in the fashionable short-waisted slashed doublet, and the *breacan an fheilidh* or belted plaid in a dense check of predominantly red tartan on a saffron ground. His outfit was idealized in contemporary Gaelic poetry.   *SNPG*

THE HIGHLAND HABIT

By 1600 the dress of all men in the Highlands was seen by outsiders as a sort of exotic uniform, in which tartan was the most distinctive element:

> ...the habite of the Highland men...is stockings (which they call short hose) made of a warm stuff of divers colours, which they call tartane...a jerkin of the same stuff that their hose is of, their garters being bands of hay or straw, with a plaid about their shoulders, which is a mantle of divers colours, much finer and lighter stuff than their hose, with blue flat caps on their heads.

In the late sixteenth and seventeenth centuries the image of the Highlander as warrior-hero swathed in tartan was born. The reasons for this involve social change within Gaelic society, changes in contemporary dress styles, and improved economic wellbeing in the Highlands due initially to the development of a trade in cattle. The opening up of the Highlands to wider influences brought the kilted Highlander to the attention of a curious and more literate audience; writers found something exotic to describe to their readers.

This opening up was part of the emergence of Europe from the upheavals of the Thirty Years War into a period when political, religious and commercial rivalry expanded dramatically. Trade and warfare were both on a larger scale than ever before, with irreversible effects on societies and individuals.

Within Highland society itself conditions were changing. The bard was the clan's main propagandist. In the seventeenth century the Gaelic poet began to look beyond the horizons of his own and neighbouring clans, and turned from a local to a national political perspective. With the Civil War and the ultimate exile of the Stewart kings clans were aligned as Whig or Tory, Presbyterian or Roman Catholic, generally depending on inter-clan politics. The bards had always composed powerful propagandist verse, an effective means of incitement in a pre-literate society. Now their songs had a political resonance that reached beyond the clans themselves.

Tartan became a stock phrase in conventional praise poetry, conveying dignity, nobility and dress-sense. It is evident from the message of Gaelic song and from the comments of observers that love of colour, attention to detail

Reconstruction by the nineteenth century artist, R R McIan, of the belted plaid worn in the seventeenth century. It shows the plaid fixed on the shoulder with a brooch. Details such as the sett of the tartan are fanciful. *NMS*

and embellishment, and appreciation of skilfully woven fabrics inspired dress in the Highlands and Islands. The Gaelic word most commonly used to describe tartan is *breacan* which referred specifically to the plaid, gathered at the waist by a belt, pinned on the shoulder by a brooch, and worn kilted on the thighs. It is based on the root word *breac*, meaning speckled.

The mantle, a basic feature of early dress, evolved into the plaid in the sixteenth and seventeenth centuries. There are many written references to plaid in this period but little pictorial evidence. George Jamesone's 'Genealogie of the Campbells of Glenorchy' reveals a little detail. Jamesone painted this vast canvas for Sir Colin Campbell, 8th of Glenorchy, in 1635. In it Sir Duncan Campbell of Lochow, the celebrated ancestor of the family, is wearing a garment of ancient origin which was described by the Latin word *chlamys* meaning 'cloak'.

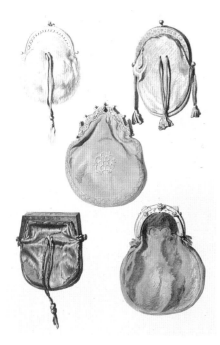

Types of early sporrans, a form of purse worn as a pouch on the belt with the belted plaid. James Drummond RSA, 1860.   *NMS*

Sir Duncan Campbell of Lochow, the founder of the Campbells of Glenorchy, sitting symbolically at the base of his family tree, painted by George Jamesone in 1635 (detail). He is wearing the 'loose cloak of several ells', fastened with a brooch at the neck and belted at the waist.   *SNPG*

EX DONO THOMÆ CALDER DE SHIRVA, MERCATORIS GLASGUENSIS.

Above: The Highlander's plaid was an ancient and widespread style of dress. The art of draping an untailored length of cloth is illustrated by this male figure in a toga on a classical stone sculpture recovered from the vicinity of the Antonine Wall. From *The Monuments of Imperial Rome discovered in Scotland* (etc) (Glasgow, about 1771).　　*NMS*

Below: A Highlander depicted by a French artist of the eighteenth century, in blue bonnet, tartan plaid and hose, demonstrating the versatility of his clothing.　　*NMS*

Above: The sari is also an example of how a substantial length of cloth can be artfully arranged.　　*Picturepoint – London*

Inverlochy Castle by Horatio McCulloch, 1857, a romantic perception of the 'Land of the Mountain and the Flood'. Viewed from the west, the painting shows the shoulder of Ben Nevis over which Montrose's Royalist army marched to victory against the Earl of Argyll in February 1645. *NGS*

Reconstruction by John Sobieski Stuart in *The Costume of the Clans* (Edinburgh 1845) of the portrait of Andrew Macpherson of Cluny dressed in the ideal costume of plaid, trews and jerkin of the late seventeenth century Highland chieftain. The outfit is worn as a riding dress with the shoulder plaid or *breacan-spreighte*. *NMS*

As the seventeenth century progresses, we learn more about tartan and Highland dress. Personal display had always been important, especially when the clans gathered for war. John MacDonald's 'A Song to Montrose', composed about 1646, describes the costume and equipment of the clans who joined Montrose. In 1689 the *Grameid* rehearses the glories of the campaign of Viscount Dundee, which culminated in his tactical triumph but death and effective defeat at Killiecrankie. The clans were drawn up in saffron array. Glengarry's men were in scarlet hose and plaids crossed with a purple stripe; Lochiel was in a coat of three colours; the plaid worn by MacNeil of Barra 'rivalled the rainbow'.

It was fashionable for the plaid to be 'kilted above the knee'. Short hose or stockings of the same tartan fabric were worn. The leg covering, of different qualities of wool and differently woven, was extended into a form of tight trouser knows as *triubhas*, mentioned in seventeenth-century references in English as 'trews'. They are described in Gaelic verse as 'carefully tailored and close fitting'. They were worn in bad weather, and were also adopted for horseback. Just as the horseman was regarded as something of a superior being, riding garb was equated with the chieftains, the leading men of the clan, and the well-to-do. It is evident that, in the late seventeenth century when more men were drawn onto the battlefields, these distinctions were emphasized.

The trews were different from other forms of trousers, and Highlanders came to regard them as a mark of distinction between themselves and Lowland Scots – and even other Highlanders, especially when referred to in satirical vein. When the Sinclairs were defeated at the battle of *Allt nam Meirleach* in Caithness in 1681 by Sir John Campbell of Glenorchy a song and pipe tune celebrated the victory. The distinctive dress of the northern clan gave rise to a volley of contempt from Campbell of Glenorchy's piper, Finlay MacIvor:

Tha bodaich nam briogais...
A nise retreuta

The peasants in trousers...are now flying before us

The plaid was also worn by women. Sir William Brereton, an English visitor to Edinburgh in 1636, described the dress of the womenfolk:

Many wear (especially of the meaner sort) plaids, which is a garment of the same woollen stuff whereof saddle cloths in England are made, which is cast over their heads, and covers their faces on both sides, and would reach almost to the ground, but that they pluck them up, and wear them cast under their arms.

This type of large shawl remained as a typical garment of Scots women. A version was the *earasaid*, or 'arisaid' in its anglicized form, worn by women in the Highlands and Islands. Especially fine examples were said to have been worn by women in the Hebrides.

In his song on the Rising of 1715 John MacDonald of Aird, Benbecula, expresses his enthusiasm for the Jacobite cause in conventionally extravagant praise of his chieftain Allan MacDonald, 14th Chief of Clanranald, and singles out the women as a particular virtue of Clanranald's Hebridean lands. He praises their beauty, set off by the *earasaid*, and describes them assembled for dancing, wearing the *breid caol*, a narrow kerchief worn by married women (unmarried women wore a fillet or ribbon, *stiom*, as a headband).

Until the middle of the eighteenth century it was the custom for every woman to wear a plaid, most commonly of tartan. Plaids or plaiding were Scots terms used to describe the relatively coarse woven twilled cloth that might be used, for example, for bed coverings as well as garments. These

The *earasaid* (or 'arisaid'), the fashionable dress in tartan for women in the Highlands and Islands before the eighteenth century. *NMS*

lengths of cloth might be in shades of white or a marled grey, or patterned in tartan. Borrowed into Gaelic the word *plaide* means a blanket, and suggests that this was originally its primary meaning in Scots. One or two centres of the emerging textile industry gained a reputation for making plaids, in particular Glasgow and Galloway. 'Glasgow plaids' were already well known in the seventeenth century.

In the 1690s Martin Martin of Skye wrote a detailed account of Highland and Island dress.

> The plaid wore only by the men is made of fine wool, the threads as fine as can be made of that kind. It consists of divers colours: and there is a great deal of ingenuity required in sorting the colours so as to be agreeable to the nicest fancy.... Every isle differs from each other in their fancy of making plaids as to the stripes in breadth and colours. This humour is as different through the mainland of the Highlands, insofar that they who have seen those places are able at first view of a man's plaid to guess the place of his residence.

Martin's account, from *A Description of the Western Islands of Scotland* (1703), suggests that the sett or design of tartan differed both according to locality and to preference of weaver and wearer. Although personal choice as to colour and style was clearly important, Martin infers that an identification with locality played a part.

Large flat seventeenth-century ring brooch of brass from Tomintoul in the highlands of Banffshire. These brooches were worn by women to fasten on the large tartan plaid. *NMS*

Kenneth, Lord Duffus, painted by Richard Waitt about 1712, wearing a belted plaid of a predominantly red, black and yellow tartan, and hose of tartan cloth. The image presented conforms to the aristocrat of Gaelic society celebrated as *sealgair sithne,* 'the hunter of deer', in clan panegyric poetry.   *SNPG*

John Campbell of Ardmaddie by William Mosman, 1749. Campbell, a lawyer and banker in Edinburgh, became the Principal Cashier of the Royal Bank of Scotland. Known to tradition as *Caimbeul a' Bhanca* 'Campbell of the Bank', he was a popular figure and the subject of a bardic tribute by the great Gaelic poet, Duncan Ban MacIntyre. Though moving in the fast stream of British commerce he also occupied comfortably the world of traditional Gaelic society and chose to have himself painted in full Highland dress of tartan belted plaid shortly after its proscription by act of parliament. He is standing against a window onto his clan territory in which Ardmaddie Bay is dominated by a cliff and the cave in which his Campbell ancestor had hidden.
Royal Bank of Scotland Collection

THE JACOBITE WARS

Even well into the eighteenth century the Highlands of Scotland remained foreign territory to most of Britain, including Lowland Scots.

> They are but little known even to the Inhabitants of the low country of Scotland for they have ever dreaded the Difficulties and Dangers of travelling among the Mountains... But to the People of England, excepting some few, and those chiefly the Soldiery, the Highlands are hardly known at all, for there has been less, that I know of, written upon the Subject than of either of the Indies; and even that little that has been said conveys no Idea of what a Traveller almost continually sees and meets with in passing among the Mountains; nor does it communicate any Notion of the Temper of the Natives while they remain in their own country.

This was written by Edward Burt, a civil engineer, on road-survey duties with General Wade's forces in the Highlands in the 1720s. But although Highland society was largely unknown the Highland fighting man was gaining a reputation as a formidable warrior whose uniform of tartan plaid made him immediately recognizable. An account of one of the actions of the 1715 Rising around Loch Lomond illustrates this:

> ...fourty or fifty stately Fellows in their short Hose and belted Plaids, and arm'd each of them with a well fix'd gun on his shoulder, a strong handsome Target, with a sharp pointed steel of above half an ell in length screw'd into the Navel of it, on his left arm, a sturdy Claymore by his side, and a pistol or two with a Durk and Knife on his belt...

To the Highlander, clothes and their style and colour, as well as weaponry, were always of great importance. This is reflected in some remarkable examples of Gaelic praise poetry, which are consistent in their specific references to tartan as the glory of Highland dress.

Different Gaelic words were used to describe the ways of wearing tartan. *Breacan* refers specifically to the belted plaid, while *eileadh*, meaning 'folding', was used to describe the kilt, suggesting that it was customarily a pleated garment. In time, the word with the addition of the letter *f* and the qualification of *mor*, 'great', or *beag*, 'small', came to denote two distinct styles of

Highlanders dressed in tartan plaids and trews showing the dress of ordinary folk whom Edward Burt met on the road while travelling in the Highlands in the 1720s. He was on road survey duties with General Wade's forces and described his experiences in *Letters from a Gentleman in the North of Scotland*. *NMS*

William Cumming, Piper to the Laird of
Grant, painted by Richard Waitt in 1714. The
piper is shown in the panoply of feudal
chieftain with banner and coat of arms,
feudal stronghold, and a form of livery with a
red and yellow (or white) tartan.   *NMS*

garment, the plaid and the kilt. *Feileadh beag* passed into the English language as 'filabeg' or 'phillabeg', made familiar by Walter Scott and others. A stock phrase in Gaelic praise poetry, *luchd nam breacanan fheilidh*, described 'the men of the pleated tartans', and was taken up by Scott and others.

In a song of the 1740s the Jacobite poet Alexander MacDonald praises the tartan plaid in rousing terms:

B'fhearr leam breacan uallach
Mu m'ghuaillibh 's a chur fo m'achlais
Na ge do gheibhinn cota
De'n chlo as fearr thig a Sasann.

Better for me is the proud plaid
Around my shoulder and put under my arm,
Better than though I would get a coat
Of the best cloth that comes from England.

Tartan house dress or gown with a full lining of blue silk, about 1770. *By courtesy of the Earl of Leven and Melville*

John Ramsay of Ochtertyre commented that the dress of early eighteenth-century Scottish gentry resembled their domestic economy, in general plain and frugal, but on great occasions sparing no expense. He commented on the ostentation of the Highland gentry, who indulged in 'expense which neither suited their ordinary appearance nor their estates' and adopting elaborate styles 'when they came to the low country'. It is evident from the household accounts of Highland families that there was a keen demand for fine textiles and trimming, supplied by tailors and merchants in burghs such as Glasgow, Inverness and Leith. The MacDonalds of Clanranald, for instance, were in the second half of the seventeenth century making regular purchases of fine cloth, lace, fancy ribbons and silver buttons.

The political events of the 'Glorious Revolution' of 1689, which brought William III to the throne, strengthened a nationalism centred on the exiled Stewart kings. Especially after the Union of the Parliaments in 1707 tartan became widely identified with this nationalism. Scott commented:

.... I have been told, and believed until now, that the use of tartans was never general in Scotland until the Union, with the detestation of that measure, led it to be adopted as the National colour, and the ladies all affected tartan screens.

In the years after the Union most of Scotland's difficulties were blamed on an 'English' government. Antagonism was expressed not only through Highland and Jacobite opposition but in Lowland discontent: the eruption of the Edinburgh mob in the Porteous riots of 1736 is an example.

Gown or housecoat of a fine silk tartan in brilliant colours described as a 'Clan Chattan' sett, worn by one of the Hays of Yester in East Lothian in the eighteenth century. *NMS*

But Gaelic culture gives a particularly vigorous expression to the sense of nationhood and opposition to an alien government and culture, as 'The Song of the Highland Clans', of about 1715, shows.

Theid maithe na Galldachd
Gle shanntach 'sa'chuis

The nobles of the Lowlands will engage
Very eagerly in the cause...

It was a traditional belief, intensified by the Union, that there would be a Gaelic or pan-Celtic revival, preceded by a national uprising in Scotland and victory in a great battle '*thall aig Cluaidh*', 'beyond Strathclyde'. Its survival since the thirteenth-century 'Prophecies of Thomas the Rhymer' was much more robust and vigorous than has often been realized. The Jacobite cause provided a new focus for this belief, and tartan gave it an easily identifiable uniform. '*Is i seo aimsir an dearbhar*,' the bard went on:

This is the time when
The prophecy will be proved for us
The men of Scotland
Are keen and spirited
Under arms at the forefront of battle
When every brave hero will rise
In his splendid new uniform
In a spirit of anger and fierceness
For the service of the crown.

Tartan suit of jacket and trews commissioned from an Edinburgh tailor for an English Jacobite, Sir John Hynde Cotton of Madingley, Cambridgeshire, when he visited Scotland in 1744. The sett of his tartan is complicated, differing considerably between warp and weft, and is unknown today.   *NMS*

Right: Barracks at Ruthven in Badenoch built strategically in 1718 to garrison the Highlands against lawlessness and civil war.   *NMS*

Opposite: Highland soldiers on the march in 1743 showing different styles of wearing Highland dress on campaign, from a hand-coloured German print. This scene, in which camp followers include wives and gillies, might have taken place on the Continent during the War of the Austrian Succession in which General Wade's Independent Companies were engaged.   *NMS*

Opposite: Tartans associated with Prince Charles Edward from his time in Scotland. A piece of tartan cut from a plaid left at Moy Hall rests on the tartan now known as Mackintosh. The background is a plaid reconstructed from surviving scraps of a 'suit of Highland cloathes' given to the Prince in Arisaig by Catriona MacDonald of Borrodale when he was a fugitive after Culloden.
NMS

The Battle of Culloden depicted by Ernest Griset after David Morier for George II, showing men of the Jacobite army dressed in 'little kilts', jackets, waistcoats and trews in which 23 different tartans can be counted.
NMS

By this time the Highland dress of tartan plaid was well known. It was worn by chieftain and clansman, by lord and man, by both sexes, and it was a symbol not only of identity but of noble virtues.

Its growing prominence arose from the involvement of Highlanders in Britain's national politics, and in the armed conflicts to which these gave rise, both in Britain and in Continental Europe. From 1639 Highlanders were recruited into the cause of the Covenants, Royalist risings and the support for the Stewart kings that resulted in the Jacobite wars. In 1745 Prince Charles Edward Stewart adopted Highland dress as a uniform for his army, and tartan became a symbol of Jacobitism. The prince was presented with a gift of Highland dress by Scottish Jacobites before 1745, and this may have encouraged his belief in the symbolic value of tartan. A striking characteristic of Jacobite songs is their insistent reference to Charles's personal appearance,

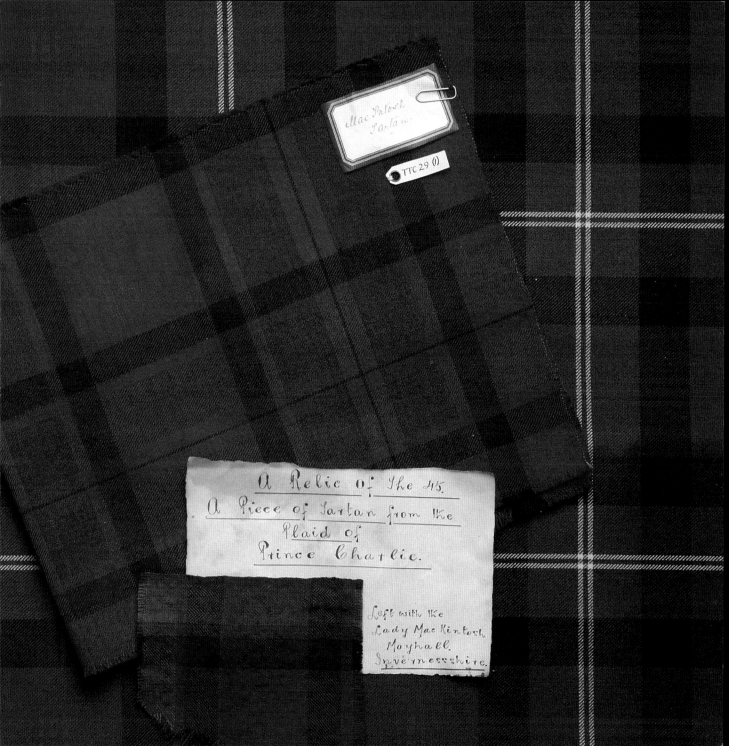

MacIntosh
Tartan.

TTC 29 (i)

A Relic of The 45.

A Piece of Tartan from the
Plaid of
Prince Charlie.

Left with the
Lady MacKintosh
Moyhall.
Invernessshire.

The strand on the Atlantic side of the island of Eriskay where Prince Charles Edward Stewart first landed on British soil on 23 July 1745 from the French privateer *Du Teillay.*   *NMS*

The Prince taking leave of the privateer captain Antoine Walsh, on reaching the mainland.   *SNPG*

his dress, and the uniforms and accoutrements of his soldiers: repeated phrases were 'bonnet blue and tartan plaid' and 'tartan trews and laigh-heeled shoes'.

Alexander MacDonald of Dalilea, the Gaelic poet, described the Prince, whom he mistook for a clergyman when he arrived in Scotland in July 1745:

> ...a tall youth of a most agreeable aspect in a plain black coat with a plain shirt not very clean and a cambrick stock fixed with a plain silver buckle, a plain hatt with a canvas string haveing one end fixed to one of his coat buttons: he had black stockings and brass buckles in his shoes.

MacDonald remembered how Prince Charlie questioned him about the comfort and convenience of the Highland dress:

> He asked me if I was not cold in that habite (viz the Highland garb). I answered I was so habituated to it that I should rather be so if I were to change my dress for any other. At this he laugh'd heartily and next required how I lay with it at night, which I explained to him; he said that by wraping myself so close in my plaid, I would be unprepared for any sudden defence in the case of a surprise. I answered that in such times of danger or during a war, we had a different method of using the plaid, that with one spring I could start to my feet with drawn sword and cock'd pistol in my hand without being in the least incumber'd with my bedcloaths.

After the debacle of the battle of Culloden, the Prince was himself a fugitive. Hugh MacDonald of Baleshare described meeting him in Uist.

> His dress was then a tartan short coat and vest of the same, got from Lady Clanranald, his night cap linen, all patched with soot drops, his shirt, hands and face patched with the same, a short kilt, tartan hose and Highland brogues, his upper coat being English cloth.

Loch nan Uamh between Moidart and Arisaig where Prince Charles Edward landed and departed from Scotland and where he was sheltered twice as a fugitive in 1745-46. *SEA*

AFTER CULLODEN

Sir Robert Murray Keith, a descendant of the hereditary Marischals to the Kings of Scots, exiled for their part in the Jacobite Wars, painted by Anton Graff in Dresden in 1770. He sits for his portrait in tailored belted plaid in dark green and black tartan.   *NMS*

The Disarming Act of 1746 outlawed the wearing of Highland dress. This was a harsh measure with harshly enforced penalties – imprisonment and transportation. The Act caused great hardship and resentment, but the strictness of the sanctions reflected the serious fear and sense of political threat inspired by tartan. The wording was unequivocal:

> That from and after the first day of August, One thousand and seven hundred and forty-seven, no man or boy within that part of Great Britain called Scotland, shall, on any pretext whatever, wear or put on the clothes commonly called Highland clothes (that is to say) the Plaid, Philabeg, or little Kilt, Trowse, Shoulder-belts, or any part whatever of what peculiarly belongs to the Highland Garb; and that no tartan or party-coloured plaid or stuff shall be used for Great Coats or upper coats, and if any such person shall presume after the said first day of August, to wear or put on the aforesaid garments or any part of them, every such person so ofending...shall be liable to be transported to any of His Majesty's plantations beyond the seas, there to remain for the space of seven years.

The penalties against the wearing of tartan and Highland dress were, for some years, strictly enforced. In 1748 a man, Mackay, was arrested in Inverness and charged with wearing Highland dress. His defence was that he had no other dress and was not aware of the law. Mackay was sentenced to six months imprisonment.

Captain Hughes of General Pulteney's Regiment, reporting from Kinlochrannoch on 15 October 1749, wrote:

> On the fifth of this month, Duncan Campbell and his son, inhabitants of Glen Falloch, were apprehended in Highland Cloaths by the moving Patrole and are confined in the Tolbooth of Killin.

There were many such arrests, but there were also problems of interpretation. Captain George Sempill reported that in Morar men were wearing 'instead of breeches, stuff trousers, much after the form of those the seamen use, but not longer than the kilt or philabeg'. He was uncertain whether to 'take notice of such people as offenders against the law'.

There was a real conviction that the Jacobite movement presented a continuing threat. In the wake of Culloden the Duke of Cumberland set in train a campaign of attrocities which earned him the title 'Butcher'. His severity was less the result of an appetite for wanton destruction than of fear of another uprising. The Disarming Act was an important step in destroying this possibility.

It was not easy even for the willing to comply. William Mackenzie of Gruinard in Wester Ross wrote to Baillie John Mackintosh of Inverness in 1748 about a market for his salmon and asked the Baillie for a copy of the Disarming Act. He added, 'As we cannot appear in our country habit any more, [you] may send me some swatches of your cloths and freeses and acquaint the prices.'

Tartan and Highland dress did not disappear from use, but dress began subtly to change. The Reverend Donald Martin, describing the state of his Skye parish of Kilmuir in 1790, wrote:

> Fifty years ago, the old Highland dress universally prevailed – hats, long coats, boots, spurs, watches etc were rare. Now every gentleman wears them; and persons of substance, of both sexes, dress as fashionably, and live in a style as elegant as those of the same rank in the southern parts of Scotland.

Skye crofters, John MacLeod and his wife, aged 73 and 70, about 1812, a portrait of folk of modest circumstances in their working clothes of homespun tweeds – not of tartan then if they ever had been. *NMS*

Highland Dance painted by David Allan, about 1780, in which pipers play for a 'Foursome Reel' near Blair Atholl. If the artist has not embellished the costume of the dancing figures, it is evident that a taste for tartan as smart wear had outlived the years of proscription. *NGS*

Jacket and waistcoat of about 1774 belonging to James Bruce of Kinnaird, the explorer. The choice of sett by a Lowland laird of fame ensured its perpetuation as the Bruce of Kinnaird tartan, named retrospectively in the early nineteenth century. *By courtesy of the Earl of Elgin*

Although styles changed 'for persons of substance', tartan itself survived.

At one time it had been common for every woman to wear a plaid, usually tartan, when she left the house. Those with wealth and a taste for fashion had plaids of silk; some wore woollen plaids lined with silk; many had to be satisfied with plain worsted, although this was often of the highest quality. In the early 1750s silk or velvet cloaks replaced the plaid, and, in the cities, the plaid soon came to be regarded as antiquated. But in country areas, both Lowland and Highland, it was not so readily laid aside. The Edinburgh wig-maker and poet, Allan Ramsay (1686-1758) railed against the change of fashion that replaced the plaid with the scarf, a fashion which he urged folk to resist strenuously.

In spite of changes in fashion there remained a respect for tartan within Highland society, and an admiration for it elsewhere. In 1791 the minister of the Argyll parish of Lochgoilhead, the Reverend Dugal MacDougall, wrote:

The inhabitants in general, except those who carry on the fishing, continue to wear the Highland dress, the bonnet, the philabeg, and tartan hose; even the authority of an act of Parliament, was not sufficient to make them relinquish their ancient garb.

In *The Clans of the Scottish Highlands* (1845 and 1847) James Logan and R R McIan elaborated on the growing myth of clan tartans while representing historical forms of Highland costume based on research. *NMS*

Highland shepherd in a late eighteenth
century style of dress adopted by shepherds
and drovers – men on the move.   _NMS_

Flora MacDonald of South Uist, a relation of
the Chief of Clanranald and one of the
saviours of Prince Charles Edward Stewart in
1746, painted by Richard Wilson in the
fashionable attire of ladies in Scotland who
sympathized with the Jacobite political cause.
SNPG

This may have been practical necessity, but it is said that there was 'a rage of wearing tartan' following the end of the Jacobite Wars. Ramsay of Ochtertyre, looking back in the late eighteenth century over more than a generation, wrote:

> The Jacobite ladies took that method of expressing their attachment to an unfortunate prince. They used tartans not only in plaids, but in gowns, riding-clothes, bed and window curtains, even in shoes and pin-cushions. The Whigs once thought of arraying the hangman in the Prince's pattern; but they did more wisely in having Whig tartan, which ere long made both parties give it over.

Among the paintings in the Royal Collection at Windsor is Du Pan's 1745 portrait group of the children of Frederick Prince of Wales and his wife Augusta of Saxe-Gotha, including his eldest son, later George III, dressed in the uniform of an Archer. The boy's coat and breeches are of a red tartan. It appears to be a fine and tightly twilled design, and if it is not a 'hard' wool yarn it may be a Catelan silk, part of the renowned patterned fabric that was such a popular export from Barcelona. The Prince's coat is a more elaborate version of the tartan coats worn by the King's Bodyguard of Archers in Scotland in the early eighteenth century. Nearly fifty years later tartan was still not identified with clanship. In a delightful study of the young brothers Sir James and Sir Alexander Macdonald of Sleat, about 1766, the different setts of tartan they wear show its insignificance as a clan badge.

After 1746 a generation grew up without the need to be warriors first and foremost, and the importance in Highland society of the fighting man declined. However, the involvement of Britain in large-scale continental wars brought a need for military manpower. Recruitment in the Highlands and Islands provided the opportunity for those of martial tendencies to perpetuate some of the old traditions.

But recruitment into the British army had begun much earlier. In 1724 Field Marshal George Wade was appointed Commander-in-Chief in Scotland with the specific task of demilitarizing the Highlands. He planted garrisons and built roads to open up the Highlands and speed the movement of troops. In addition, he formed six 'independent companies' of Highlanders in 1725, each one to police the area from which it was recruited, and to counter any suspected Jacobite activity. The recruits were to come from all parts of the Highlands, but in practice they tended to be drawn from Whig clans, such as Campbells, Grants and Munros.

These independent companies wore the Highland dress of belted plaid, and when in 1739 they were formed into a regiment of ten companies they were

James 5th Earl of Wemyss in his uniform of the Royal Company of Archers painted about 1715.   *Royal Company of Archers*

Charles Campbell of Lochlane painted in full Highland dress about 1760. He was an advocate and member of the pro-Hanoverian faction in Scotland. His predominantly red tartan is of an unknown sett but the bright colour was fashionable and prestigious. *SNPG*

Sir James MacDonald of Sleat and Sir Alexander MacDonald painted by Jeremiah Davison about 1766. This study of the MacDonald children shows the insignificance of tartan as a badge of clanship – four different setts can be distinguished on the garments worn. The tartan jacket of the left hand figure was the basis of a MacDonald Lord of the Isles sett created in the nineteenth century.   *SNPG*

The bridge over the Tay at Aberfeldy designed by William Adam in 1732 provides the background to the monument commemorating the muster of the Black Watch in 1739. The bridge was celebrated in Gaelic tradition as one of the three 'Wonders of Scotland'.   *Patricia Macdonald*

supplied with a uniform tartan of 'government pattern' in a green, blue and black check. The regiment was called the Black Watch, their name recalling the 'watch' employed by clans to guard against cattle raiding. The uniform of Highland infantry in the late eighteenth century consisted of kilt and plaid of government tartan (Black Watch), red coat, red and white hose, and black buckled shoes. Regiments were distinguished not by clan tartans but by facing colour, that is, the colour of the material used to trim the coats at collar and cuffs.

At this time there were many more Highland line and fencible regiments which saw active service all over the world. Artists and engravers produced prints in great numbers to supply a market keen for images of the Highlander. The number of pictures of Highland soldiers surviving from this period is out of proportion to their overall numbers in the armed forces.

John Murray, Earl of Dunmore, painted by Sir Joshua Reynolds in 1765, showing a contrast between a popular bright red tartan and a dark government pattern of broad green and blue bands.   *SNPG*

Hugh Montgomerie, Earl of Eglinton, painted by John Singleton Copley, in the uniform of the Black Watch with 'government pattern' kilt and red tunic coat with green facings.   *SNPG*

Highland soldier in government service wearing the belted plaid and using an upper corner to keep the lock of his musket dry. *NMS*

Swatches of 'government tartan' based on a loosely specified military sett of dark green, blue and black of the early eighteenth century. Highland regiments adopted the military tartan with modifications, the Gordons with an overcheck of yellow, Seaforths with an overcheck of red and white. Absolute uniformity with exact numbers of thread counts of each of the colours was almost certainly unknown in the eighteenth century when the regiments were formed and the strictness of specification for a military sett is uncertain since red tartans were also worn by men in the government service. *NMS*

Neil MacLean, Piper to the Highland Society of London, about 1785, dressed in livery at the Society's expense, including kilt, detached plaid, sporran, pistol, red coat and waistcoat. The portrait by William Craig demonstrates how ideas on 'full Highland dress' as formal costume had evolved at a comparatively early date.   *NMS*

Colonel William Gordon of Fyvie painted in Rome by Pompeo Batoni in 1766. The subject's plaid is reminiscent of a Roman toga and he is set in a classical landscape.
National Trust for Scotland

REVIVAL

This is bringing before all the sons of the Gael that the King and Parliament of Britain have for ever abolished the Act against the Highland Dress that came down to the clans from the beginning of the world to the year 1746. This must bring great joy to every Highland heart. You are no longer bound down to the unmanly dress of the Lowlanders. This is declaring to every man, young and old, simple and gentle, that they may after this put on and wear the trews, the little kilt, the doublet and hose, along with the tartan kilt, without fear of the laws of the land, or the spite of enemies.

These words are from a proclamation written in Gaelic and posted up in the Highlands in 1782. In that year the Marquis of Graham, afterwards the Duke of Montrose, introduced the bill to repeal the Act of 1746. It was passed without a dissenting voice. The Marquis was hailed as a hero in Scotland.

Gaelic poets called for a celebration and a return to tartan and the 'lightsome plaid' – *am breacan uallach* – but the act of restoration was little more than symbolic for most Highlanders. Some felt strongly about the lifting of proscription and returned to tartan, kilt and plaid. Many did not have the resources to make a choice, for it was a time of dearth and famine in most of the Highlands.

Migration from the Highlands in the second half of the eighteenth century brought a growth of Gaelic-speaking communities in Edinburgh and Glasgow. In 1769 the Gaelic Chapel opened in Edinburgh's steeply sloping Castle Wynd. The poverty-stricken state of agriculture in the Highlands and growing opportunities for employment in Edinburgh's expanding New Town, had encouraged large numbers of Highlanders into the city. They were not a vociferous element in the urban population primarily because English or Scots was not their first language, but their spiritual welfare was taken very seriously.

Their understandable attachment to their homes, in spite of change and decline, gave rise to support for issues of principle, such as the restoration of tartan. In succeeding generations this became a nostalgic embrace of the traditional culture of the Highlands, real or imagined. The publication of

The exotic appearance of this late eighteenth-century portrait reflected contemporary fascination for the well-dressed 'gentleman' drover who had grown rich in the rising market of the cattle trade. Tartan was his trademark. *NMS*

the poetry of James Macpherson of Badenoch in the 1760s encouraged this. The poetry, presented as translations of the poems of Ossian, inspired an unprecedented interest in the Highlands and Gaelic culture. They caused a long-running literary fracas over the character and antiquity of the poems and, more usefully, laid the foundation of serious scholarship in Gaelic literature.

Not only Highlanders but the outside world scrutinized this traditional culture. For non-Gaelic speakers, Jacobite song or balladry, of which more

Sir Alexander MacDonald of Sleat, a figure of the European Enlightenment shown in full Highland dress in about 1775 in a green tartan that was later chosen as the exclusive tartan of the Chief of Clan Donald.   *SNPG*

Locket with miniature portrait of Prince Charles Edward Stewart wearing Highland dress of tartan short coat and the Ribbon and Star of the Order of the Garter. Wine glass, about 1775, with an enamelled portrait of Prince Charles Edward Stewart used to celebrate the Prince's birthday. Silk white cockade, the badge of Jacobite adherence in 1745-46.   *NMS*

was composed in the late eighteenth and nineteenth centuries than during the Jacobite Wars themselves, put much of this sentiment and nostalgia into winning words.

The outside world identified tartan with Jacobitism and the cause of the exiled Stewarts, but in Gaelic tradition a ribbon, rosette or patch of white silk or other fabric had been the recognized badge of the Jacobites. It is evident from many sources that tartan itself did not distinguish friend from foe; the wearing of a white or black cockade was the most important mark of identification. The Gaelic poet, William Ross, in an elegy on the death of Prince Charles Edward in 1788, uses the White Cockade, *An Suaithneas Ban*, as the embodiment not only of Prince Charlie but of an old Scotland whose ruin was symbolized by the death of the Prince.

Carved wooden shop sign of a Highlander taking snuff designed to advertise the sale of snuff and tobacco. Because in the eighteenth century Scots were famous for taking snuff, the figure of an officer in a Highland regiment was adopted as the symbol of the trade. *NMS*

Soraidh bhuan do'n t-Suaithneas Bhan
Gu latha luain cha ghluais o'n bhas;
Ghlac an uaigh an Suaithneas Ban
Is leacan fuaraidh tuaim a thamh.

A long farewell to the White Cockade,
Till the day of Doom it will not move from the state of death;
The grave has taken the White Cockade,
And cold slabs form the tomb in which he rests.

This is the last genuine Jacobite song and the Prince's only true elegy, entirely free from the unreal sentiment of Lowland Jacobite balladry.

But outside the Highlands tartan remained the most overt symbol of this 'primitive' Gaelic culture. Gaelic society itself preserved or appropriated tartan for more subtle and deep-seated reasons. Some well-known Scottish portraits of the seventeenth, eighteenth and nineteenth centuries show Highland subjects portrayed in traditional dress, armed and accoutred in the traditional manner, against the background of their own *duthaich* or family and clan territory. An example is Jeremiah Davison's portrait of Alexander MacDonald, 8th Baronet of Sleat, a widely travelled and educated figure of Enlightenment Scotland, portrayed as a Highland chieftain.

Symbolic gestures were not only captured in paintings. When in 1787 the act proscribing the MacGregors was repealed Joseph MacGregor, the first minister of the Gaelic Chapel in Edinburgh, dressed himself in a full suit of the MacGregor tartan and walked conspicuously about the city. It was a possibly dangerous act and it raised eyebrows, but even the cultivated city of Edinburgh was well used to such sights, and had been since its occupation by the forces of Prince Charles Edward in the autumn of 1745.

Trade token issued by an Edinburgh tobacconist in 1796 showing a Highlander in what was described as the 'Gallant Garb of Scotland'. It suggests that war service had saved tartan and Highland dress and encouraged its adoption as a symbol of national identity. *NMS*

THE HIGHLAND REGIMENTS

Grenadiers of the 42nd and 92nd Highlanders in their uniforms of the British Army of the Napoleonic Wars, showing the extent to which Highland dress had evolved its military uniformity by 1812, differing only in details such as a red overcheck on the government tartan and the facings on the tunics. *NMS*

With the outbreak in 1756 of the Seven Years War with France there was an urgent need to raise new regiments. William Pitt, George II's prime minister, saw the recruitment of Highlanders as a means both of destroying 'disaffection' and gaining good soldiers. 'I sought for merit wherever it was to be found,' he said later, '...and I found it in the mountains of the north. I called it forth and drew it into your service, an hardy and intrepid race of men.'

The adoption of tartan as the uniform of the Highland regiments helped them to be accepted and to gain recruits. And the success of the troops themselves, who established a resounding reputation at home and overseas, effectively popularized tartan. The tartan-clad Highland soldier encouraged the creation of the Gael as the embodiment of Scotland and of past heroism:

> ...when the Highland regiments proved themselves among the finest material in the British Army, so that the Nobility sought the honour of command in them, what might have come to be regarded as the barbarous if picturesque dress of a bygone age remained to acquire an aura of military glory.

The legislation proscribing Highland dress had made an exception for those serving in the Army. The Highland regiments wore the uniform of the 'Government Pattern', a dark tartan of green, blue and black in which distinguishing lines of red, white and yellow were added for different regiments. The Cameron Highlanders were the first to break with this convention, when on their formation in 1793 they invented a tartan of their own. The Regiment was raised in Lochaber by Alan Cameron of Erracht. It was thought that the prevailing red colour of his tartan would not harmonize well with the scarlet coatee then worn, and at the suggestion of his mother he adopted a 'MacDonald' tartan for the regiment, omitting three of the thin red lines in it and adding a yellow stripe from his own tartan.

Any disenchantment about military life among Highlanders was muted, and failed to disturb a growing adoration of tartan. It enjoyed the full attention of fashionable society again, now reflecting contemporary admiration for its military character. Ladies in the cities wore feminized versions of military uniform. The artist John Kay satirized these fashions in one or two of his cartoon portraits. His 'Military Promenade' of 1795 shows the Misses Maxwell in the tartanized uniform of the West Lowland Fencibles, of which their father was Lieutenant Colonel.

As tartan gained a hold on fashion attention was focused on questions of historic detail. Whether the trews or the kilt were the authentic traditional dress of the Highlander was hotly debated. The engraved diploma for the Highland Society of London offered a compromise, with a crest that showed both styles. The crest was designed in 1805 by Benjamin West (1738-1829), an American by birth, who became President of the Royal Academy in 1792.

In a celebrated portrait of 1794 by Raeburn, Sir John Sinclair of Ulbster, President of the Highland Society, is wearing the uniform of the Rothesay and Caithness Fencibles, of which he was the Colonel Commandant. Sir John had designated trews as the correct wear for the regiment, and the most ancient form of Highland dress. As a prominent politician and agriculturalist, and the moving force behind the *Statistical Account*, the survey of parishes

Silver medal by Benjamin West commissioned by the Highland Society of London in 1801 as a tribute to the 42nd Regiment and their part in General Abercrombie's victory at Alexandria. The Highland soldier easily fulfilled the role of classical warrior.   *NMS*

Diploma for the Highland Society of London by Benjamin West in 1805. The design reflects a compromise in the contemporary debate as to the antique form of Highland dress. One of the crest's supporters is in kilt, plaid and feather bonnet, the other in tight-fitting trews.   *NGS*

Portrait of a young officer of the Seaforth Highlanders, about 1854, in the theatrical form of uniform known as 'Review Order'. Highland dress was highly susceptible to the elaboration demanded by Victorian taste and a showpiece army.   *NMS*

throughout Scotland, Sir John was a man whose opinions were not to be taken lightly.

But accurate knowledge about traditional dress was fragmentary, and before the nineteenth century was the preserve of a purely oral tradition. Opinion on the trews varied. A well-known dance takes its title from the garment described as 'old trews', *Seann Triubhas*. It was a lively tradition that this was the only dance that Highlanders would condescend to perform in the styles of dress allowed under the terms of the Disarming Act. Others have claimed that the dance was a celebration of the Act's repeal in 1782.

When in Scott's *Waverley* the Baron of Bradwardine congratulates Edward Waverley on the figure that he cut when fully attired as a Highlander he remarked, 'Ye wear the trews, a garment whilk I approve maist of the twa, as mair ancient and seemly', and the narrator adds that Waverley had now fairly assumed the 'garb of old Gaul'.

Ministers writing about their parishes at the end of the eighteenth century in the *Statistical Account* give the impression (often highly subjective) that Highland dress, especially the kilt, was common in the countryside, but in the towns was worn only on special occasions. Alexander Campbell, the schoolmaster of Portree commented in 1794:

The philibeg is rarely wore, except in summer and on Sundays, on which days, and some other occasions, those in better circumstances, appear in tartans, a bonnet, and short hose, and some in a hat, short coat, waistcoat, and breeches of Scotch or English manufacture.

In fact, tartan was being adopted as a kind of livery. In the nineteenth century livery became more entrenched and more dramatic. Portraits commissioned by wealthy patrons, such as Queen Victoria, the Earls of Breadalbane and the Dukes of Atholl, show a new race of piper-servants of the Highland estates. They are in more elaborate gear, the style and detail depending on fashion or the tastes and aspirations of employers. Several of these pipers are commemorated in portraits.

It was largely due to the Highland regiments that Highland dress survived, and its classification for military use laid the foundations for later designs and the tendency towards uniformity. These developments and growing feelings about authentic pedigree prompted serious research and, significantly, the initiative came from those who had departed their native heath.

Captain or Company Officer of the 5th (Deeside Highland) Volunteer Battalion of the Gordon Highlanders. Much of the volunteers' *esprit de corps* derived from an identity with locality and clan tartan, here the distinctive Gordon with yellow overcheck on the traditional military sett of the eighteenth century. The watercolour portrait is by the military artist E A Campbell (1879-1951). *NMS*

Veterans of the Crimea campaign photographed on their return to Britain at Queen Victoria's request. These Seaforth Highlanders in bright red Royal Stewart tartan and scarlet tunics had gone into battle in these uniforms. *NMS*

RESEARCH AND RE-CREATION

Gregor MacGregor, aged 84, veteran of the 42nd Highlanders, Balquhidder, Perthshire, about 1812. The prestige of military service meant that this old soldier habitually wore the kilt but this was undoubtedly unusual for everyday wear. *NMS*

Research into tartans and Highland dress was initiated by the Highland Society of London whose first public effort was towards the repealing of the Disarming Act itself and the legal reinstatement of tartan. The Society was founded in 1778, with objectives that were philanthropic as well as cultural. The founders, concerned at the decay in Highland social and economic life, aimed to protect and encourage Highland dress and music, and Gaelic language and literature. They also cared for the needs of expatriate Highlanders, war veterans, widows and orphans, as well as taking steps to improve agriculture and encourage economic effort in the Highlands themselves.

The Society began its collection of tartans at a time when interest in tartan and its history had grown considerably. In 1815 a member of the Society suggested that a collection be made from the clans and leading families to encourage their interest in tartans and to save the old patterns from being lost. Since Highland dress had been outlawed for more than a generation the older arts of dyeing and weaving tartan were disappearing. The Society then wrote to the chiefs and heads of families and asked them to 'furnish as much of the tartan of their clans as will serve to show the patterns'. An extract from the Secretary's letter to Colonel Macdonnel (*sic*) of Glengarry reads:

The Highland Society of London instructed me to apply to the Chiefs of the different Clans and request them to transmit to me as much of their respective Tartans as would be sufficient to show the Pattern and to authenticate each by attaching a card having on it the impression of their respective Coat of Arms. I have to beg that you will be so obliging as to forward me about a yard of the real Glengarry Tartan – authenticated in the manner mentioned. No time is to be lost as I am sorry to say that all the Cean Cinne do not feel by much the Highland Spirit by which you are animated and in a few years it is to be feared that the distinguishing Tartans of some Clans will not be known.

Between 1816 and 1820 about forty samples were submitted, many of them sealed and certified in writing by the clan chiefs. These were sewn into a folio ledger which is preserved in the Society's archives.

The Collection of Certified Tartans grew steadily during the nineteenth century. It has been admired by scholars and all those concerned with Highland history and the preservation of tradition. The Collection evolved in stages. In the 1930s it was reorganized into two new volumes containing Highland tartans only, with Lowland tartans being kept separately. The new arrangement included examples of old hand-woven tartans from a collection made in Skye. More recently it has continued to grow and diversify.

Within twenty years distrust of the Highlands became fascination. The influence of Macpherson's Ossian was amplified by the poems and novels of Scott, but there was clearly a powerful attraction in tartan itself. Its essence is display, and George IV's visit to Scotland in 1822, an event stage-managed by Scott, was the occasion of much exposure. The manufacture of tartan then became a commercial success, and began to affect fashion in London and Paris. Tartan was in vogue, and has remained so ever since.

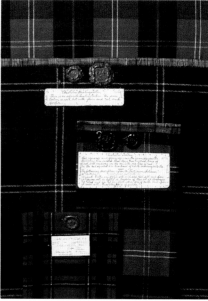

Tartan samples collected by the Highland Society of London in the nineteenth century and endorsed and sealed by the donors, in this case the chiefs of Chisholm whose solemn belief in the antiquity of their tartan was based on its creation by the Sobieski Stuarts in *Vestiarium Scoticum*, 1842.   *NMS*

Macbeth and his men in costumes of tartan, created by John Martin. The facts of eleventh-century Scottish history were absorbed by the fiction required to satisfy nineteenth-century taste.   *NGS*

French hand-coloured engraving caricaturing the exotic qualities of Highland soldiers observed with fascination in Paris in 1816 after the Battle of Waterloo.   *NMS*

George IV had a lifelong interest in the martial arts and in arms and armour, which he collected assiduously. His imagination was stirred by the Highlander as warrior-hero, a beau-ideal fulfilled for him by the young Reginald George MacDonald, 20th Chief of Clanranald. A contemporary observer noted:

We have the best authority for stating that his Majesty's partiality for the tartan was not formed in Edinburgh. For several years past Clanronald has been wont to appear at court in Highland garb, and his Majesty uniformly expressed his decided approbation of the dress, and of the chief who wore it. On one of these occasions, when Clanronald appeared in the full costume befitting the chief of the Macdonalds, his Majesty received him most graciously, and presented to him a magnificent broad-sword, which the City of Glasgow gave to Prince Charles. His Majesty's words to Clanronald on that occasion were 'I will always be happy to see you *in that dress*'.

The visit of George IV inspired a new zeal for Highland history and tartan. Groups of Highlanders gathered in the capital under the command of their respective chiefs. An Edinburgh citizen spoke for many when he commented 'Sir Walter Scott has ridiculously made us appear to be a nation of Highlanders, and the bagpipe and the tartan are the order of the day'. This did not cool the fervour for ceremony. The chiefs vied with each other over the splendours of their retinues, and memories were searched for the setts and colours of a tartan tradition which seemed to have disappeared.

Prominent amongst the clans were the MacGregors, still with memories of being outlawed. Lieutenant Alexander MacGregor of the Royal East Middlesex Regiment of Militia, and a scion of the Black House of Fernan and the MacGregors of Roro, acted as adjutant of the detachment of Clan Gregor under the chiefship of Sir Evan Murray MacGregor. 'The party of the Clan numbered fifty armed with swords, pistols, targets and sporrans, and in the Highland Dress of Clan Gregor.' It had the honour of escorting the Regalia of Scotland from Edinburgh Castle to Holyrood Palace for the King to view.

When George IV stepped ashore in Leith and progressed to Edinburgh it was the signal for a prolonged and extravagant ceremony. It was pure theatre of a kind that had been outlawed in Lowland Scotland for about two hundred years. Totally unexpected but suitably dramatic was the arrival of Alasdair Ronaldson MacDonnell of Glengarry at the gallop. The histrionic subject of Raeburn's portrait, fully clothed in tartan, reined up at the king's state landau, swept off his bonnet and proclaimed, 'Your Majesty is welcome to Scotland!'

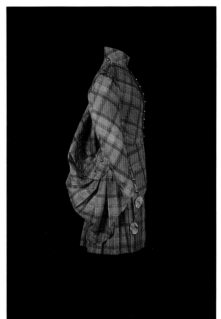

Costume in hard tartan made probably for George IV's visit to Scotland in 1822. The outfit, including a close-fitting jacket cut on the bias, exudes style and flamboyance and a sense of personality. The sophisticated tailoring includes a light plaid separate from the kilt but designed and worn to resemble the traditional unsewn belted plaid.   *NMS*

Mac Mhic Alasdair, Colonel Alasdair Ronaldson MacDonnell of Glengarry, painted by Sir Henry Raeburn in 1812, striking a pose in his ancestral hall as traditional leader of Gaelic society. His dress is nevertheless in the latest fashion of Regency coat, 'little kilt' and separately tailored plaid. The dark tartan is unlike any MacDonald tartan known today.   *NGS*

Jacket, kilt, plaid and sporran. Highland dress as costume, about 1835.   *NMS*

Silk tartan dress of the 'Clan Chattan' sett, the trousseau of Sara Justina Davidson of Tulloch, about 1832.   *NMS*

J M W Turner's painting 'March of the Highlanders' seems to inaugurate the emerging career of national image and stereotype. Against the dramatic backdrop of Edinburgh Castle rock and buildings of the Old Town, hundreds, if not thousands, of Highlanders are seen on the march. They are swathed in kilts and tartan, accoutred with swords and targes, and spurred on by pipers: by a sleight of hand, the image and the myth are born.

'Highland dress' turned into 'tartan costume'. A practical dress with style became in the nineteenth century a fashionable dress with little regard for function. Some styles were reasonably faithful to history – for example the adaptation of the simple untailored plaid into styles for men and women. But from the 1820s new styles evolved based on the interpretation of an imagined past, reinforced by strict conventions of dress. The old 'hard' tartans of finely combed yarn and dense twill were augmented by softer Saxony cloth and the lightness and lustre of silk. From the 1840s royal patronage encouraged the Victorian endorsement of Scotland, and Highland dress, tartan dresses, jackets, shawls and sashes became high fashion in Britain, France and beyond.

Tartan soon had its historians, and armed with their information canny producers soon led the market. Bannockburn, near Stirling, was by the eighteenth century a well-known centre of weaving and textile manufacture. One family, the Wilsons, began to dominate this cottage industry and over the next century were mainly responsible for creating tartan as we know it today.

The earliest records of the Wilson family go back to 1765 but there is a family tradition that they began in business in 1724. They travelled widely through Scotland to find new patterns as well as to market their wares: it is ironic that they established their reputation for tartan during the period between 1747 and 1782, when tartan was proscribed. Much of what they produced went to provide uniforms for the Highland regiments.

In the weaving pattern books of Wilsons and in their orders of the late eighteenth century the tartans are described by numbers only. Some were known by names no longer used, and only a very few by clan names. The setts and shades were assembled according to changing demand, and not to a set of rules as they now are. A sample book of 1820, for example, shows a selection of sett designs which includes 'Durham', 'Smallest 42nd', 'Robin Hood', 'Clarke', 'Eglinton', 'White Wellington' and 'Large Gipsy'.

Names of tartans and clan associations had origins that were probably in most cases more commercial than historical. Wilsons of Bannockburn made, for example, a tartan called 'New Bruce' which subsequently became the

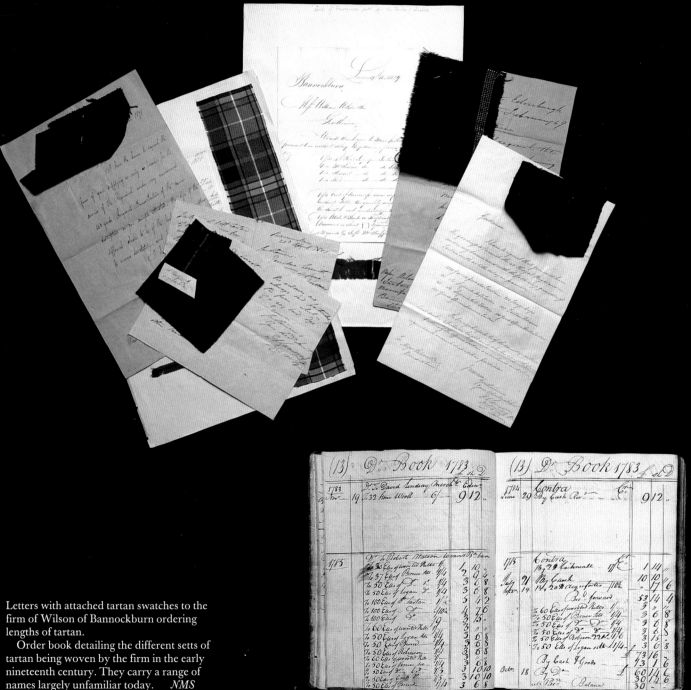

Letters with attached tartan swatches to the firm of Wilson of Bannockburn ordering lengths of tartan.

Order book detailing the different setts of tartan being woven by the firm in the early nineteenth century. They carry a range of names largely unfamiliar today. *NMS*

LE MONITEUR DES DAMES ET DES DEMOISELLES

Hand-coloured engraving as an advertisement for Paris fashions in the 1880s. *NMS*

Grant tartan. We do not know anything of the pedigree of this sett beyond this expedient of name change. They may have found an old tartan and given it a name, randomly, or a Grant may have chosen to wear it and so conferred on it a new identity.

Aristocratic patronage always provided a touchstone of authenticity and the Highland nobility and gentry were keen to provide what they regarded with confidence as the correct answer. Thus they colluded in the commercial process. A letter to Messrs Wilson and Sons of February 1818 tries to endorse correct styles and tartan.

> Gentlemen
>
> Your favour of yesterday I have received and in reply, the Dress that the Duke of Atholl wore at the meeting of the Highland Society lately in this place was a Black Coat and Star, Black Vest, Black small clothes and Black Silk Stockings, but you will please observe that this meeting his Grace attended was one of what is called the true Highlanders, being a branch of the Inverness Society, whereas the Perth Gaelic Society none can attend their Anniversary meetings without being dressed out in the real old highland Garb – the Duke of Atholl however has a Tartan of his own which must be well known to you under the name of the Atholl Tartan.
>
> > I am Gentlemen
> > Your most obdt.
>
> M. Stewart.

The technical problems of ensuring a continuous supply, as much as the dictates of taste, persuaded Wilsons to standardize their product and to give each type a specific name. From 1819 they began to regularize the setts and to lay down exact thread counts. Many tartans were designed, and given a name if they proved popular. Some were altered several times until they caught the attention of the public.

After George IV's 1822 visit Wilsons of Bannockburn could not satisfy the demand for tartan, and every piece was sold immediately it came off the loom. They opened a new weaving mill, named 'The Royal George', and for a while their best selling lines of tartan were 'King George the Fourth' and 'Sir Walter Scott'. This was the period when the so-called 'fancy tartans' began to be manufactured, and names such as 'Caledonia' and 'Wellington' appear in Wilsons' records.

The trade wanted tartan in thousands of yards and was frequently impatient. 'Any new Patterns' were requested, and tartans were produced to order. Setts were enlarged or reduced as fashion dictated, and in many cases enhanced by thin red, yellow and white lines woven in silk. The tremendous enthusiasm for tartan in turn inspired books whose researches attempted to explain the history of tartan. Notable were James Logan's *The Scottish Gael* of 1831 and the Sobieski Stuarts' *The Costume of the Clans* of 1845, which excited the contemporary imagination without resolving the confusion of variety. These books caused considerable controversy over their sometimes imaginative reconstruction of the past, but they kept tartan before the public eye and Wilsons of Bannockburn in business.

By the mid-nineteenth century competitors had entered the field of tartan weaving, and tartan contracts for the Army had been divided by the War Office. Wilsons of Bannockburn diversified into tweed and carpet weaving during the second half of the century and continued in business until 1924.

Right: A Seaforth Highlander officer of 1815, modern Dresden porcelain.   *NMS*

The Thin Red Line by Robert Gibb RSA, 1881. 93rd Highlanders in Sutherland tartan in action at Balaclava, 1854.   *United Distillers*

CREATING HISTORY

As the enthusiasm for tartan grew, ideas about its history and antiquity as well as a system of clan associations were codified by a small group of authors. Working from scant facts, a colourful and elaborate history was created, with an aura of romance tailored to the demands of the contemporary imagination.

The Sobieski Stuarts' *Vestiarium Scoticum* was published in 1842 and the related volume *The Costume of the Clans* in 1845. These books established and consolidated the clan associations of tartan and ascribed specific clan identity to nearly all setts or designs. The authors, a legend in their own right, rested their case on sixteenth-century manuscripts which they claimed to have discovered. These established a medieval origin for clan tartan. These documents have since been discredited and, unfortunately and mistakenly, much of the rest of their work tends to be dismissed.

John and Charles Hay Allan appeared in Scotland in about 1820, claiming to be the long-lost grandsons of Bonnie Prince Charlie. They could not have arrived at a better time. They were hospitably received, and set up in primitive splendour on the Lovat estates, where they learnt Gaelic and diligently researched Highland history. Known as the 'Sobieski Stuarts' these eccentric but talented brothers produced work that seemed plausible. But although there were many supporters for *Vestiarum Scoticum* it was doubted by scholars. Sir Walter Scott's opinion was conclusive. He was quoted as saying that 'the style and dialect of the specimen shown him were utterly false, a most feeble and clumsy imitation of the writing of the period'.

In 1826 the young Aberdonian James Logan collected in the Highlands a wealth of information of antiquarian interest. He turned this into his aptly-named *The Scottish Gael, or Celtic Manners as preserved among the Highlanders* (1831), which contained the first extensive and detailed essay on tartan. In an appendix he listed fifty-four tartans which he could authenticate. To these he added tables with the design of each tartan with its colours and proportions. This was one of the most sound of early histories, and its enthusiastic reception spurred Logan on to further essays.

He collaborated with the artist Robert Ronald McIan to produce the

Highland cavalier created by the veteran patriot Theodore Napier, about 1900, the costume including belted plaid, tartan hose and deerskin brogues. Photographed by Hill and Adamson. *SNPG*

Opposite: Swatch of early nineteenth-century hard tartan in the sett that later came to be firmly established as Stewart of Appin. Though an old sett whose design and colours were consistently popular, it was never the exclusive property of one clan. *NMS*

Right and below: Reproductions from a Jacobite print of a chieftain (1714) and a standard bearer (1745) by the Sobieski Stuarts (*Costume of the Clans*, 1845). Though the figures are extravagant, such jackets, waistcoats, bonnet feathers and tailored hose were popular, and the tartan belted plaids are also credible.
NMS

John Sobieski Stolberg Stuart in a calotype portrait by Hill and Adamson. John and his brother Charles Hay Allan were renowned as the long-lost grandsons of Prince Charles Edward, and they creatively dressed the part. *SNPG*

sumptuous two-volumed *The Clans of the Scottish Highlands* between 1845 and 1847, elaborating on the myth of clan tartan and providing fictions as compelling as any facts. Logan was for a short time Assistant Secretary to the Highland Society of London, and acknowledged the patronage and support of the Society in the publication of these volumes.

The Highlanders of Scotland, published in 1870, combined the growing historical interest in the clans with an interest in Highland dress. The artist, Kenneth MacLeay, was commissioned by the Queen in 1865 to prepare the watercolour portraits. At that time the Queen could write, 'I think the Highlanders are the finest race in the World.' Undoubtedly, the portraits, with a commentary by Amelia Murray MacGregor, reflect this view.

Illustration for the first detailed historical analysis of tartan by James Logan in the quaintly-titled *The Scottish Gael, or Celtic Manners as preserved among the Highlanders* (1831). The portraits, though fanciful, were honest attempts to re-create traditional Highland dress of the period before proscriptive laws.   *NMS*

JOHN CHISHOLM.
GLEN CANNICH,
ROSS-SHIRE.
CLAN CHISHOLM

COLIN STEWART CAMERON.
NEWTONMORE,
BADENOCH
INVERNESS-SHIRE.
CLAN CAMERON.

JOHN CAMERON.
MUCCOMER,
LOCHABER.

Triple portrait of 1864 by Kenneth MacLeay for his series of royal retainers and men of the principal Highland clans as commissioned by Queen Victoria. Kilts were now elaborately tailored with an apron front and the back sewn into neat pleats.   *NMS*

ROYAL ENDORSEMENT

One of the more significant ingredients in the success of tartan was its endorsement by royalty during Queen Victoria's long reign. The ownership of Highland estates reminded her of a remote but tangible connection with the ancient dynasty of the Royal House of Stewart, of the 'king over the water', and Bonnie Prince Charlie's desperate and hopeless bid for the throne. This was a heady mixture.

Under Victoria and Albert tartan gained international renown. Women's and children's clothing, high style, tartan souvenirs and tartan interiors reflected the domestic life of the royal family's Scottish retreat at Balmoral. Specialized forms of tartan were developed to suit different occasions, and added 'hunting' and 'dress' setts to existing clan setts. New aniline dyes made the designs more vivid than ever.

Opposite: By the late nineteenth century the setts of the Scottish tartans had become fixed in their designs and thread counts. The designs in this group were genuinely old but their categorical naming as Murray of Atholl, Fraser of Altyre and MacColl was a modern process. *NMS*

Flora MacDonald watching over a sleeping Prince Charles Edward with two Highlanders as look-outs, acted out in tableau-vivant at Balmoral on 6 October 1888 and recorded by the Aberdeen photographer George Washington Wilson. *AAGM*

Queen Victoria's enthusiasm for the Highlands and Highlanders was fired by her first visit to Scotland in 1842. She described in her journal the arrival of the royal party at the massive baronial pile of Taymouth Castle on the evening of Wednesday 7 September 1842.

The *coup d'oeil* was indescribable. There were a number of Lord Breadalbane's Highlanders, all in the Campbell tartan, drawn up in front of the house, with Lord Breadalbane himself in a Highland dress at their head, a few of Sir Neil Menzies' men (in the Menzies red and white tartan), a number of pipers playing, and a company of the 92nd Highlanders, also in kilts. The firing of the guns, the cheering of the great crowd, the picturesqueness of the country, with its rich background of wooded hills, altogether formed one of the finest scenes imaginable. It seemed as if a great chieftain in olden feudal times was receiving his sovereign. It was princely and romantic.

The romantic imagination, besieged by a thrusting industrial society, thirsted for the spectacle of primitive splendour. The Earl of Breadalbane had organized a ceremonial welcome exactly suited to the taste of his generation. It was, of course, something of a distraction from the pitiful conditions suffered

Queen Victoria, Prince Albert and royal retinue fording the River Tarff in Glen Tilt, painted by Carl Haag in 1861.
Windsor Castle, Royal Library.
© 1990 Her Majesty The Queen

in the 1840s by many Highland communities, particularly in the Hebrides, then in the throes of clearance, famine and epidemics. And it was the beginning of financial ruin for Lord Breadalbane's family.

The Queen and Prince Albert acquired the castle and estates of Balmoral on Deeside. Amongst later additions to the property was the Forest of Ballochbuie, which tradition tells was bought by the Farquharsons from the MacGregors for a tartan plaid. When Victoria bought the Forest in 1878 she raised a stone there inscribed with the words, 'The bonniest plaid in Scotland'.

Balmoral was an extravagant interpretation of Scottish vernacular forms of architecture. Parts of the interior, especially the Queen's own suite of rooms, were decked with tartan. The bright red of the Royal Stewart and its green Hunting Stewart counterpart were used for carpets, and Dress Stewart for curtains and upholstery. The Queen herself favoured a variation of the Royal Stewart tartan in which the broad band of red is changed to white, similar to the design given in the *Vestiarium Scoticum* as 'Royal Stewart'. This Dress Stewart was also called 'Victoria'. Prince Albert was much involved in the castle and its arrangement, and his interest led him to design a tartan, first produced in about 1860 for the exclusive use of the royal household.

Boy's tartan costume made in Paris in 1871. *GMAG*

The Balmoral tartan was personally designed by Prince Albert in the 1850s. The sett was based on the so-called 'Royal Stewart' but in shades of marled grey to represent the rugged Grampian peaks.   *NMS*

Silk tartan gown, about 1865, in the sett known as 'Dress Stewart' popularized by Queen Victoria and the ladies of the Royal Household.   *NMS*

Souvenir ware of wood decorated with a printed tartan made by the family firm of W and A Smith of Mauchline, 1820-1860. *NMS*

Opposite: The accoutrements of the Victorian soldier's uniform had developed in pace with the enthusiasm for finery and detail in Highland dress. The pedigrees of plaid and brooch, dirk, sporran, and belt plate were respectable but the interpretation was imaginative.   *NMS*

An attempt in 1881 to abolish regimental tartans in the interests of economy and uniformity was resisted by a petition prepared at a dramatic meeting of the Scottish aristocracy at Stafford House in London. 'Tampering with the Tartan' was their rallying cry.   *NMS*

Newly created conventions favoured as full a range of accoutrements as possible, now largely decorative rather than functional. A fine example of such decorative additions is displayed in the Scottish Tartans Museum in Comrie: it is a purpose-made chest of accoutrements that belonged to the Irvine Robertson family of ministers and Gaelic scholars from Atholl. It includes a complete ensemble of a pair of pistols, powder horn, dirk, sgian dubh, sporran, shoe buckles, plaid brooch, and bonnet badges.

Tartan itself proliferated. Trinkets and souvenirs, such as snuff boxes, tea caddies, pirn boxes, spectacle and card cases and wooden buttons, were decorated with tartan designs and became increasingly popular.

Finlay, deerstalker in the service of Walter Frederick Campbell of Islay, about 1845, in a calotype portrait by Hill and Adamson. The old tradition of the clan chieftain's retinue was perpetuated in the dressing of Highland estate employees in the laird's tartan or tweed.   *SNPG*

Demand for tartan both at home and abroad was keen, and the textile industry was tooled up to supply it. Tartan was a typical exhibit in the great contemporary international exhibitions. In the Glasgow International Exhibition of 1888, for example, there were exhibits from one of the many tartan warehouses. The catalogue entries were finely tuned to the Victorian taste for history and tradition. While speculating on the antiquity of tartans, the authors commented:

> ... some critics go the length of saying that while Tartans in themselves may be old, the distinctive patterns to which clan names are attached are only an affair of the day before yesterday and cannot be traced further back than the early part of the present century. This view is too absurd to require refutation.

Day dress of closely-fitted skirt and bodice of the 1880s, styled to Victorian taste in Carnegie tartan. *NMS*

Tartan used as the fabric to enhance Edwardian fashion in an advertisement from the Paris fashion houses. *NMS*

Hand-coloured cartoon by the French fashion artist, George Barbier, in his 1922 series of '*Falbalas et Fanfreluches*'. His sensuous interpretation of the pastoral ideal took the tartan-clad Highlander as the romantic poet, a bizarre sequel to the cultural tragedies of nineteenth-century Scotland. *NMS*

The evolution of Highland costume by the late nineteenth century, tailored in this case in Robertson tartan for evening wear. *NMS*

Donald MacDonald, Kinagarry, Arisaig,
photographed by Miss M E M Donaldson
about 1910. He is dressed in tattered re-made
garments representing the twilight of tartan
as everyday wear of Highlanders.   *SEA*

George MacDonald, Bunacaimb, Morar,
photographed by Miss M E M Donaldson
about 1910. It was then unusual for country
folk to possess Highland dress of such
quality, but as a successful piper he had the
wardrobe compulsory for competition piping
in the nineteenth and twentieth centuries.
SEA

The enthusiasm continued into the twentieth century. In about 1902 *Comunn an Fheilidh* (The Kilt Society) was founded, based in Inverness, and firmly stating its purpose to encourage and perpetuate the wearing of Highland dress, to remove prejudices against the kilt, and to gather and interpret information on how Highland dress should be worn. The Society held its annual general meeting in Inverness on the Thursday of 'Wool Market' week, symbolically appropriate and designed to capture as large a Highland membership as possible – the Wool Market was one of the busiest social events of the Highland calendar. The Society canvassed opinions on the wearing of the kilt from leading Highland chiefs and noblemen '...in whose families the Kilt has been worn for centuries'. The views expressed by the officers of the Society summarized precisely contemporary attitudes to and knowledge about tartan.

No dress worn by the inhabitants of Britain has a more ancient, romantic and honourable history than the Highland dress, and yet it has been the plaything of fortune from its earliest days.

Tartan suit in the MacDonald Lord of the Isles sett made for the Duke of Windsor. This is a rendering of the tartan worn by Sir Alexander MacDonald of Sleat in a late eighteenth-century portrait and claimed as of right by the Prince of Wales in the 1930s as pertaining to the title of Lord of the Isles forfeited to the Crown in 1493.   *By courtesy of Mohammed Al-Fayed*

The creation of tartan for individuals, families, societies and corporations has been a busy process over the last 150 years. Highland roots are an advantage but not a necessity as the Hannays have shown.   *NMS*

The Kilt Society played its part in confirming a created history of tartan. This history has been shaped by an interpretation of the past that is peculiarly modern. Another influence has been the application of heraldry to tartan. The Lord Lyon began to enforce rigorous standards of registration of tartan designs, regarding the judgment of tartan as part of his jurisdiction as 'Badges and Signs of Recognition whatsoever borne or used by the Clans'. A list of registered tartans was included in *The Clans, Septs and Regiments of the Scottish Highlands* of 1907. If a tartan were to be used as such it had to be approved by the Lord Lyon, and if approval were not granted the sett remained a 'plaid' and was not to be called a tartan.

Such rules have maintained the standards created in the nineteenth century and imbued tartan with a special quality derived from history but not organically part of it. It is valid in the context of its invention, but has little or no validity in the remote past and the rich tradition in which tartan truly belongs. The world's response to tartan, as a bold, attractive and incomparable design, has taken tartan beyond the borders of tradition. But from the souvenir to high fashion it conveys a message of national identity, and throughout the world that message says Scotland. There is no other pattern like it.

Take the ingredient of tartan and add to any image to give distinctive identity and sense of history.   *Murray Grigor, Scotch Myths Archives*

Ensemble dubbed 'Highland Spirit' by its designer Yves St. Laurent. Though an exuberant creation, the tone is traditional with a bright bold tartan design on a skirt with full pleats like a kilt, a military tunic of black velvet trimmed with gold braid, and a velvet bonnet with large feathers like a seventeenth century chieftain. Even the most independent of modern designers remains faithful to 'the Highland habit' of old.
Arthur Elgort, for Yves Saint Laurent Rive Gauche

THE TARTANS

This selection of ancient and modern tartans tells the story of the principal clans and families that have dominated Scottish history since the middle ages. Most of these names belong to the Highlands and Islands, where tartan was worn traditionally and acted as a mark of distinction, a fact commented on frequently in the historical literature. There are many colours and designs, and it was natural that there should be local and regional variations in tartan in a country divided by mountains and seas, and by clan loyalties and conflicts. But authentic old tartan does not survive in any quantity because its fabric is by nature frail, and the close association of tartan with name and clan is difficult to make before the early nineteenth century.

Though tartan is today regarded as a badge of Scottish clanship this was not always so. There were no clan tartans as such at the time of the Jacobite War of 1745, for example, and Alexander MacDonald, the Gaelic poet, relates how it was impossible to distinguish his own Clan Ranald MacDonalds from other MacDonalds, such as Sleat, by their breacan or tartan; this could only be done from the badges in their bonnets. However, since its first mention in the fifteenth century, 'tartan' has been part of the decorative art of dress, and the word was used to describe quality cloth with its ornamental characteristics of colours woven in stripes and into rich checks. In this sense it has a noble and ancient pedigree. Today it is also a mark of genealogy and descent, since it is now an established tradition that we distinguish the different 'sets' with the names of chieftains, families and clans. Yet, while individuals and groups can claim a tartan to wear to proclaim their pedigree and descent, they are also wearing a badge of nationhood and proclaiming a firm sense of belonging.

Acknowledgement: The tartan swatches were kindly lent by the Clan Tartan Centre of James Pringle Weavers, through the good offices of James McAslan.

Bruce

Bruce is one of the most celebrated names in the history of Scotland, introduced by Norman followers of David I in the 12th century. King Robert the Bruce drove the English out of Scotland after the Battle of Bannockburn in 1314. A coat and waistcoat worn by the famous explorer, James Bruce of Kinnaird, in the late 18th century, has provided the tartan adopted by the family and name.

Buchanan

A highly-coloured tartan is worn by the Buchanans from the district of that name on the shores of Loch Lomond. They received their clan territories from the powerful medieval earls of Lennox, for whom they probably acted as churchmen. Their name is the Gaelic *both-chanain*, 'the house of the canon', signifying that they were dignitaries of the Celtic church. The chief of Buchanan's ancestor was Absalon, and many of his descendants took the name MacAuslan.

Cameron

The Cameron clan belongs to Lochaber and the Great Glen in the West Highlands where they held their lands of Loch Eil and Loch Arkaig by the sword for centuries. Other families such as the MacMartins, MacSorleys, MacMillans and MacPhies were brought under their control under the leadership of chieftains such as Allan of the Forays, the Great Ewen and the Gentle Lochiel – the chief of the clan customarily taking his title from his lands of Loch Eil. They were active in support of the exiled Royal House of Stewart and, as the Cameron Highlanders, in supporting the present line of British kings and queens.

Campbell

An old Campbell tartan in green was adopted as the uniform of the Black Watch in the 18th century. The clan were known in Gaelic as *Siol Dhiarmaid*, 'the race of Diarmad', the legendary Ossianic hero who fell in love with the wife of Fingal. The chieftains were customarily known as *MacCailein Mor*, 'the son of big Colin', who was the original recipient of grants of land in return for supporting the king of Scots in the Wars of Independence. By astute political action as well as by force, the Campbell clan became one of the most powerful in Scotland, with the widest territories, covering most of Argyll.

Campbell of Breadalbane

As Campbell rule expanded in the later middle ages, one of the most important extensions of territory was east into Glenorchy and Breadalbane. They created a separate branch of the Argyll Campbell family based on the imposing stronghold of Kilchurn on Loch Awe, later at Taymouth. The Breadalbane estates were so vast that by 1900 the chieftain could ride more than one hundred miles from east to west without leaving his own land. The tartan, originally probably a district tartan, was used as the uniform of the Breadalbane Fencible Regiment from 1793 to 1802.

Carnegie

The family takes its name from the barony in Angus. It is an east coast clan whose chiefs became earls of Southesk. James Carnegie, the 5th earl, supported the exiled Royal House of Stewart in the 1715 Rising and was the hero of the song *The Piper o' Dundee*. He wore as his tartan a version of the MacDonnell of Glengarry tartan, still worn today. One of the most celebrated of the name was Andrew Carnegie (1835-1919), the Scottish-American multimillionaire.

Chisholm

The sons of King Malcolm Canmore were reared under Norman influence and introduced the feudal system in the 12th century. The Chisholms, a Norman family settled in the Borders, had moved into the north east Highlands by the mid-14th century and have come to be identified with Strathglass in Inverness-shire. Their chief is known in Gaelic as *An Siosalach*, 'the Chisholm', and is said to be one of three people in the world to be accorded a definite article – the King, the Pope and the Chisholm.

Davidson

The Highland Davidsons were members of a confederation of clans known as Clan Chattan in Lochaber, Badenoch, and Strathnairn, all claiming descent from a traditional ancestor *Gille Chatain*, 'the servant of St Catan'. Their tartan, with its simple green-black-blue foundation, is a good example of the context of fashion in which tartan developed. It is named as Davidson in pattern collections used for Highland dress worn for the visit of George IV to Scotland in 1822. It is much the same pattern as the Henderson tartan.

Douglas

This is one of the most famous of the Border clans, taking its name in the 12th century from the Douglas Water in Clydesdale. Douglas was a supporter and close friend of Robert the Bruce in the wars against England and the family subsequently played a major role in medieval Scottish history when, ultimately, their power threatened the rule of the Crown. One branch became dukes of Buccleuch and Queensberry. Their tartan is an example of one created as a result of an increasing demand for named patterns in the 1820s.

Drummond

The clan was associated in the earliest historical records with the old Celtic earldoms of Lennox, Menteith and Strathearn on the southern fringes of the Highlands. There is a family tradition that their chief organised the scattering of caltraps (spiked balls spread on the ground) to stop the English cavalry at Bannockburn in 1314. The tartan is similar to the Fraser and Grant tartans and reflects the process of tartans being adopted by families and clans in the early 19th century, especially after the royal celebrations of George IV's visit in 1822.

Farquharson

This clan is descended from a historical person. It was founded by the sons of the *Fearchar Mac an Toisich*, a Shaw who was closely related to the Macintoshes and the confederation of Clan Chattan in the north east Highlands. The clan came into its ancestral territory of Braemar in the late 14th century as keepers of the King's Forest. Their green tartan is apparently based on the Black Watch with the addition of red and yellow lines.

Forbes

The clan takes its name from the barony and lands of Forbes on Donside in Aberdeenshire. The leading families of the name still live in the north east and have owned or built some of Scotland's most beautiful castles, including the remarkable Renaissance tower of Craigievar. The Forbes tartan was probably designed in the early 19th century by changing the yellow line of the Gordon regimental tartan into a white line, thus recognising an allegiance with their neighbours and medieval rivals for supremacy in the north east Highlands.

Fraser

The clan is descended from one of the successful Anglo-Norman families brought into the Highlands by the kings of Scots; the name, or nickname, is said to derive from the French *fraise* 'strawberry'. Their chieftains are always called *Mac Simidh*, 'the son of Simon', a christian name that has been in the family since its earliest mention in historical records in 1160. A popular Fraser tartan is the Hunting Fraser, based on one of the historical setts with the red ground changed to brown.

Gordon

The Gordon name was taken from their earliest territory in Berwickshire, and from a Norman family the clan grew to be one of the most powerful in the Highlands, with lands in Lochaber and Badenoch, and in Strathbogie and Deeside in Aberdeenshire. Like the Campbells and the Mackenzies, the Gordons profited greatly from the power vacuum left by the forfeiture of the Lordship of the Isles, and their chiefs were several times appointed King's Lieutenant in the north. Their tartan was the Black Watch, with a yellow line added to make a new regimental tartan in 1794.

Gow

Gow or MacGowan (*Mac a' Ghobhainn*), the 'son of the Smith' was a name associated with Clan Donald and Clan Chattan, both powerful kin confederacies by whom the art of the metalworker was highly valued. In folklore, the descent of the Gows is traced from Hal o' the Wynd, the blacksmith who played a decisive role in the clan battle on the Inch of Perth in 1396. The simple green and blue on a red ground is an old design seen in the breeches and hose of the famous fiddler Niel Gow (1727-1807), painted by Raeburn.

Graham

The Grahams are descended from members of the Anglo-Norman aristocracy of the 12th century. They married into the family of the Celtic earls of Strathearn and acquired lands by Loch Lomond and Loch Arklet. They played a significant role in Gaelic history when the Marquis of Graham, later the 3rd Duke of Montrose, led the debate in parliament to repeal the laws against tartan and Highland dress in 1782. Two of the greatest commanders of Highland clans were James Graham, Marquis of Montrose, and John Graham of Claverhouse, 'Bonny Dundee'.

Grant

The clan is descended from a Norman-French family, settled in the Highlands during the medieval feudalisation of Scotland, and becoming a Gaelic clan under the strong influence of the society that surrounded them. Their lands in Strathspey were organised as a regality conferring powers of life and death on the chieftain, the Laird of Grant, and when he assembled his clan in the early 18th century he ordered them to wear a uniform of red and green tartan plaids. But a series of early portraits of members of the Clan Grant shows a variety of pattern and colouring in the tartan worn.

Gunn

The clan took its name from a Viking ancestor, Gunni or Gunnar, who lived in Orkney in the 12th century. They later inherited lands in the earldoms of Caithness and Sutherland. Their tartan is comparable to the Mackay tartan, one of the other northern clans. By the late 18th century they had lost most of their territories, but founded a Clan Gunn Benevolent Society in 1821 to look after the welfare of any of the name of Gunn who needed material support.

Lamont

Lamont was a Norse-Gaelic chieftain holding lands in Cowal in the early 13th century and was descended from the original Scots of Dalriada. The clan was involved in the ruthless politics of 17th-century Scotland and was massacred by the Campbells in 1646, partly for their support of the royalist cause, but also because of their involvement in an earlier invasion of Campbell territories by Alasdair 'Colkitto' MacDonald. Their tartan is closely comparable to Forbes and Campbell as all their territories were absorbed by the earls of Argyll.

Lindsay

The Lindsays were another Anglo-Norman family established in Scotland in the 12th century, this time in the vast hill district of Crawford in Clydesdale. By the mid-14th century, they had married into the native Clan MacDuff and MacDougall, Lords of Lorn, and had acquired the Highland district of Edzell and much of Angus, creating a Lordship traditionally known as the 'Land of the Lindsays'. As earls of Crawford, they took precedence over other earldoms. Their baronial castle of Edzell with its pleasure garden stands at the mouth of the Cairnamounth Pass through which Highland raiding parties moved.

MacAlister

Mac Alasdair, 'son of Alister', is a usual Highland name but the West Highland clan specifically traces its descent from *Alasdair Mor*, younger son of Donald of Islay, Lord of the Isles. Donald was son of Ranald son of Somerled, leader of the Norse-Gaelic peoples of the Hebrides in the 12th century. Appropriately, the MacAlisters belonged in the heart of the Lordship territories, in Kintyre. Their tartan is one of the true red tartans belonging to the MacDonald group, although more complex in detail, like several older tartans.

MacAulay

The *Clann Amhlaidh* belongs in Dumbartonshire and Lewis. Some of the kindred appear in the early 13th century at Ardencaple as vassals of the earls of Lennox, and others, with Norse ancestry (their name being a Gaelicised *Olaf*), belong to Uig in the west of Lewis. They supported the Norse clan of the MacLeods in their rule of much of the Outer Hebrides between the mid 14th and early 17th centuries, and in their vigorous suppression of the other local clan, the Morisons of Ness. The MacAulay tartan was designed in the early 19th century but is clearly based on older patterns.

Macbean

The clan name now represents several kin and families whose original Gaelic names indicate descent from different ancestors such as *Mac Maol Bheatha*, 'son of the servant of life' or *Mac Bheathain*, 'son of Beathan'. The *Clann Mhic Bheathain* or Clan MacBean played a prominent part as a member of the confederation of Clan Chattan. Their ancestral lands are Kinchyle, on the southern shores of Loch Ness.

MacDonald of Clanranald

The Clanranalds were one of the most important branches of Clan Donald, taking their name from Ranald, son of John of Islay, the son of Angus of Islay, supporter of Robert the Bruce and descendant of the 12th-century Norse-Gaelic leader Somerled who drove the Norse from the Scottish mainland. The clan held vast territories between the Great Glen and the Outer Hebrides including the 'Rough Bounds' between Loch Duich and Ardnamurchan, some of Lochaber and the Hebridean Uists and Small Isles. The chiefs of Clanranald were consistently patrons of the most ancient arts of the Gael and sustained the cultural traditions of the Lordship of the Isles after its forfeiture in 1493.

MacDonnell (MacDonald) of Glengarry

The clan name in this form closely reflects the original Gaelic patronymic *Mac Dhomhnaill*, 'son of Donald', used by Angus, Lord Islay in the late 13th century. The MacDonnells were a younger branch of Clanranald and their chieftains have been styled *Mac Mhic Alasdair*. The tartan is the dark MacDonald tartan with the addition of a white line.

MacDonald of Keppoch

The Keppoch MacDonalds inherited part of the Lordship of Lochaber granted by Robert the Bruce to his supporter Angus Og of Islay. Their acquisition of ancestral lands was in the Gaelic tradition of entrusting strategic territories to sons with a reputation for bravery and hardihood. The founder was Alasdair Carrach who received lands in Glen Spean and Glen Roy, taking the designation from *Ceapach* where the River Roy joins the Spean. They were notable for holding onto their lands of Brae Lochaber for centuries without a charter, or 'sheepskin title', to them.

MacDonald of Sleat

The MacDonalds of Sleat in Skye were descended from Hugh, half-brother of John, the last Lord of the Isles, who gave him Sleat in Skye in the late 15th century. Bardic tradition consistently regarded the 'children of Hugh', *Clann Uisdein*, as the senior line of Clan Donald in their descent from a prehistoric past.

MacDougall

Dougall was the eldest son of Somerled, King of the Isles, who gave him the Lordship of Lorn in Argyll. Dougall or Dugald is Gaelic *Dubh Gall*, 'dark foreigner', a Gaelic name applied to groups of Vikings who invaded Ireland and the Hebrides in the 9th century and later. Somerled and his family were typical of the mixed Norse and Gaelic stock who occupied the West Highlands and Hebrides in the medieval period. Their principal castle was Dunollie which has been compared to the Castle of Bergen in Norway. The MacDougalls' opposition to Bruce led to forfeiture and their Highland power was thereafter greatly reduced.

MacDuff

Clan MacDuff appears in historical sources of the early 12th century as one of the old Gaelic and Pictish lordships. Consequently it is the oldest and most senior of Scotland's clans; its chieftains were earls of Fife who ruled most of the eastern Highlands and were connected with the earliest historical kings of Scotland. This status has been given recognition by the heraldic red lion on gold on their coat-of-arms. Their ancient pedigree was confirmed by their central role in consecrating and enthroning the Scottish kings at Scone. Their tartan is the same as the Royal Stewart but without the white and yellow lines.

MacEwan

The clan is descended from the original Scots of Dalriada but is typical of families and clans who lost their position in Argyll in the face of Campbell expansion. They retained their traditional status because they performed the role of bards and historians to the Campbell chieftains. Their tartan compares closely with the Campbell tartans and is based on the green with blue and black bands, with a red line in place of a white.

MacFarlane

This clan lived within the old Gaelic earldom of Lennox, with lands around Arrochar and Loch Long and with a traditional gathering place at Loch Sloy. *Togail nam Bo*, 'Lifting the Cattle', is the well known MacFarlane pipe tune and the full moon was proverbially referred to as 'MacFarlane's lantern'. Their tartan is a complex of colours against a red background, though an early 19th-century source, the *Vestiarium Scoticum*, gives them a tartan of a black and white check, as simple as the red tartan is complicated.

MacGillivray

The tartan of the clan is a characteristic Clan Chattan tartan; the MacGillivrays were members of that confederation of clans. Their principal residence was Dunmaglass in Strathnairn. Their chief led Clan Chattan at the Battle of Culloden and died having cut his way through two lines of government soldiers. The original of the name may have been in Mull and Morvern where *Clann 'ic Gille Bhrath* are found as leading churchmen in the medieval period.

MacGregor

Clan Gregor has the Gaelic motto *Is rioghail mo dhream*, 'My race is royal', and like one or two other clans claim descent from Kenneth MacAlpin in the 9th century. Their emblem was the pine. Their ancestral lands in Glenorchy, Glenstrae and Glen Lyon were absorbed by the Campbells in the 15th and 16th centuries, and Clan Gregor were turned into outlaws for 150 years. Their survival is one of the dramatic stories of Highland history and one of their great names, Rob Roy, is commemorated in the simple and ancient tartan of red and black check.

MacInnes

The clan take their name from the Gaelic *MacAonghais*, 'son of Angus', possibly a 7th century leader of Dalriada. They were one of the Gaelic clans of the western mainland associated in tradition with the early endeavours of Somerled against the Vikings. Their ancestral homeland was Ardgour and Morvern with their principal residence at Kinlochaline, said to have been built by a lady of the Clan. Another family, recognised as the 'Clan Innes', created the Barony of Innes in Morayshire.

Macintosh

The clan takes its name from *Mac an Toisich*, son of the leader, and the earliest *Toiseach* was probably a thane of early feudal society. Tradition associates the clan with the Clan MacDuff and earldom of Fife, giving them the royal red lion on gold on their coat of arms. The early history of the clan describes their lands in Lochaber with their headquarters at Torcastle on the Lochy, later extending eastward into Badenoch. For many generations they were leaders of Clan Chattan, the confederation of clans acknowledging descent from *Gille Chatain* 'the servant of St Catan'. Their tartan is undoubtedly an ancient one of red with green stripes flanked by blue.

Macintyre

The clan wears what is probably a district tartan, originating in the Glenorchy area of Argyll. Its blue and green stripes on a red ground look ancient. The name, *Mac an t-Saoir*, 'son of the joiner' or 'wright', is associated with Glen Noe in Lorn, and they appear consistently as supporters of the Stewarts of Appin. One of the clan's greatest sons was Duncan Ban Macintyre, the Gaelic poet, born in Glenorchy, who fought on the government side in the '45 but displayed the traditional Gaelic loyalty to the Royal House of Stewart.

Mackay

The clan appears to have already existed in strength in the early 15th century when its chief was confirmed in his possessions by Donald, Lord of the Isles. Their ancestral lands were in the north west corner of Scotland between Caithness and Cape Wrath. This region has always been known in Gaelic as *Duthaich Mhic Aoidh*, 'the Mackay Country', implying immemorial occupation and ownership. Their tartan is blue and black on a green ground and is comparable to that of their northern neighbours, the Gunns.

Mackenzie

This powerful clan was founded by a name ancestor Kenneth in the late 15th century. They were vassals in Kintail of the Lords of the Isles, later profiting from the downfall of the Lordship and moving to richer lands in Easter Ross. Their support of the government of the kings of Scots brought them territorial control of much of the northern Highlands and the Island of Lewis. Their tartan was the regimental uniform of the Seaforth Highlanders, raised in 1778, and is based on the Black Watch with the addition of white and red lines.

MacKinnon

The plant badge of the clan is Columba's Flower and family tradition associates them with St Columba as abbots of Iona in the Age of the Saints during the 7th and 8th centuries. Their ancestral territories were lost to the MacLeans in the 14th century, and they then established themselves in Skye where they served the Lords of the Isles in a judicial capacity in the Council of the Isles.

MacLachlan

Clann Lachlainn took its name from *Lachlann Mor* who held lands in Cowal and about Loch Fyne in the 13th century and who gave his name to the district of Strathlachlan. Though their property became the Barony of Strathlachlan, their power was overshadowed by the Campbells of Argyll who, in spite of MacLachlan's support of the exiled Stewarts in the Jacobite wars, ultimately protected the family from ruin after the '45.

MacLaren

The clan claims descent from *Labhrann* or Lawrence, a 13th-century churchman whose custodial lands in Strathearn and Balquhidder became the ancestral territories of the clan. *Creag an Tuirc*, 'the boar's rock', in Balquhidder, was the traditional gathering place of the clan. Their tartan resembles the green and blue setts of other Atholl clans and appears to have been adopted by the MacLarens in the 1820s.

MacLean

The clan claims traditional descent from a name ancestor, *Gill' Eathain* of the Axe, and from the kings of Dalriada, and original occupation of lands in Morvern. Their chief received lands in Mull from the Lord of the Isles who was loyally supported by the MacLeans. Their principal stronghold has been the curtain-wall castle of Duart overlooking the Sound of Mull and they enjoyed a noble reputation in Gaelic society as generous patrons of the Gaelic arts. After the downfall of the Lordship, the MacLeans feuded with the MacDonalds in the 16th century for the control of Islay, and then drew the enmity of the increasingly powerful Campbells of Argyll who eventually succeeded in expropriating the MacLean chieftains.

MacLeod of Harris and Skye

The MacLeods were one of the western clans descended from Viking leaders of the Norse kingdom of the Isles established in the 11th century. MacLeod tradition traces ancestry to a younger son of Olaf the Black, King of Man and the Isles, who founded the two branches of the clan, *Siol Thorcuil* in Lewis (which they held until the early 17th century) and *Siol Thormaid* in Harris and Skye with a principal residence at Dunvegan which has been occupied continuously by the same family for the last seven centuries. The clan tartan with red and yellow lines on a green-blue-black ground is certainly an old one and appears in early collections.

MacLeod

It is appropriate that such a large clan which has done so much for Gaelic culture in the past should claim a second tartan and one of such a bold colour. The alternative MacLeod tartan is a good example of the creativity of tartan designing and naming in the early 19th century. It appears first in the *Vestiarium Scoticum* with its 'three black stripes on a yellow field' and was the creation of the authors, the Sobieski Stuart brothers, about 1829.

MacMillan

The clan derives its name ultimately from the Gaelic *Mac Ghillemhaoil*, the 'son of the tonsured one's servant', indicating a prestigious association with the early church in the Highlands. Their ancestral lands in Knapdale, Argyll, suggest a connection with the medieval Gaelic Lordship of the Isles. The tartan is a good example of tartan evolution and design. Red and yellow lines of the 'dress' tartan, itself an early 19th-century creation, have been superimposed on the blue, black, and green base, typical of so many of the traditional darker tartans.

MacNab

Mac-an-aba means 'son of the abbot', and clan tradition demonstrates descent from the hereditary Abbots of Glendochart in Perthshire, themselves the heirs and kinsfolk of the celebrated Celtic churchman of the 7th century, St Fillan. Their tartan is notable for its crimson and scarlet tones and was probably designed in the early 19th century.

MacNeill

The name ancestor of the clan, *Nial*, lived about the turn of the 14th century and the clan became established first in Knapdale and islands such as Colonsay in the Inner Hebrides, and subsequently in Barra in the Outer Hebrides. Their island fortress of Kismul in Castlebay is a stark reminder of the importance of sea-power in the middle ages and of the reputation of the Barra MacNeills as corsairs and pirates.

MacPhee

The MacPhees were a Hebridean clan whose name was originally identified with a Gaelic name *Dubh-sidh* or 'dark one of peace'. The chieftain originally held the island of Colonsay, serving the medieval Gaelic Lordship and sitting on the Council of the Isles, and acting also as custodian of the Records of the Lordship. The clan tartan is probably a recent creation and, appropriately, seems to be a variant of one of the red MacDonald tartans whose design is itself based on a portrait.

Macpherson

The name *Mac a' phearsain*, 'son of the parson', has been widely used since pre-Reformation times. The principal kindred of the name are distinguished by the Gaelic *Clann Mhuirich*, a clan who held lands in Badenoch and were the descendants of a certain Murdoch who probably lived in the 14th century. Their chief has traditionally been known as Macpherson of Cluny, their home near Laggan Bridge. The clan tartan as now worn is a good example of 19th-century creative design, bearing comparison with the Royal Stewart.

MacQuarrie

The clan's name is derived from the Gaelic *Mac Guaire*; *guaire* means 'proud' or 'noble', and the clan, like the MacKinnons, is probably descended from Celtic churchmen settled in Mull and Iona in the early years of the Lordship of the Isles. Their tartan is related in design to one of the older red MacDonald tartans.

MacRae

The clan name is Gaelic *Mac-rath*, 'son of good fortune', and their ancestral territory has been for centuries in Kintail in Wester Ross. Noted as archers and fighting men, they were allied to the Mackenzies in some of whose lands they lived. They fostered many Mackenzies and were customarily constables of the stronghold of Eilean Donan on Loch Duich. The MacRae tartan claims, fairly, to be an ancient one and carries the tradition that it was worn by Prince Charles Edward in 1745-46.

Matheson

The clan is descended from one of the old families (with a 12th-century origin) living within the Mackenzie territories of Lochalsh in Wester Ross. Their name, Gaelic *Mac Mhathain*, 'son of the bear', suggests a totemistic belief in early Gaelic society. Their tartan is a good example of early 19th-century tartan design.

Menzies

Though a Highland clan, the name originated with Norman-French families introduced into Scotland by the kings of Scots in the 12th century and later. The Menzies held lands in Atholl and were based at Weem near Aberfeldy. Their tartan is a familiar red and white sett whose simplicity suggests antiquity.

Morrison

This is a clan name adopted by Highland families of the north and west whose Gaelic surnames - *O Muirgheasain* and *Mac Gille Mhoire* - indicate differing ancestries. Some Morrisons are descended from a family in Lewis who were hereditary brieves or judges of the Lordship of the Isles. The tartan is a recent design but remains faithful to a northern tradition by differencing the Mackay tartan with a red stripe.

Munro

The clan territory is in the fertile lands on the Cromarty Firth in Easter Ross. Foulis Castle is their principal residence. The founding kin may have originated in Ireland but eventually opposed the pan-Gaelic leadership of the Lords of the Isles. The clan was notable for the numbers of Munros who served as professional soldiers in the European wars of the 17th century. The Munro tartan was probably created in the early 19th century, but some clansmen wear the Black Watch since several Munros were officers of the Independent Companies which later formed the Regiment.

Murray

The clan takes its name from the early Celtic kingdom of Moray, which resisted the kings of Scots in the 12th century. The leadership of the kin passed to Anglo-Norman families introduced by the Scottish kings and subsequently played a leading role in the Wars of Independence. The clan consolidated its position in Highland Perthshire in the 17th century by marriage into the earldom of Atholl and since 1703, the Murray chiefs have been dukes of Atholl. The clan tartan may well have been an Atholl district tartan before becoming the Murray tartan.

Ogilvy

The family and clan take their name from the barony of Ogilvy in Angus and their ancestors, who were sons of the Celtic earldom of Angus, first used the name as a surname in the early 13th century. Their principal residence was the 'Bonnie Hoose o' Airlie'. Their tartan is complex and was known at the turn of the 19th century as 'Drummond of Strathallan' before the two families became linked by marriage.

Ramsay

The family is descended from the Anglo-Norman followers of the 12th-century kings of Scots. Their support of Robert the Bruce in the Wars of Independence ensured their survival and their senior representatives became earls of Dalhousie in the early 17th century. Their tartan is based on the early MacGregor tartan and many MacGregors adopted the name and sought the protection of Ramsays in the period when repressive laws were enforced against the former.

Robertson

The Highland clan is well known also as *Clann Donnachaidh*, the 'children of Duncan', who were descended from hereditary abbots of Dunkeld and drew status from their dynastic association with the Celtic church. The name ancestor, Duncan, was a friend of Robert the Bruce and led his clan at the Battle of Bannockburn; the Barony of Struan in Perthshire was created for his grandson, Robert, in 1451. The clan then took its surname from this chieftain.

Ross

The clan takes its name from Ross, the old county and former earldom. Their first chief is claimed to have been *Fearchar Mac an t-Sagairt*, 'Farquhar the priest's son', descended from the hereditary abbots of Applecross and recipient of the earldom of Ross from the king of Scots in about 1230.

Scott

The surname Scott first appears in documents of the 12th century and, since it was a natural attributive for those living in Scotland or natives of Scotland living away from home, it became one of the better known names of the Border country and emerged in the later middle ages as the great Border clan of that name. The tartan appears first about 1829 and has all the character of a Highland tartan. An alternative Scott tartan in black and white was said to have been adopted and worn as a Lowland shepherd's plaid by Sir Walter Scott in 1822.

Shaw

The Highland family and clan claim descent from a leader who was a younger son of the earl of Fife and had joined the king of Scots in his conquest of Moray in the late 12th century. The son of 'Shaw' was also known as *Mac an Toisich*. Their name in Gaelic derives from *Sitheach*, an old word for wolf. The Shaws were members of Clan Chattan, the confederation of clans in Badenoch, and held the extensive hill country of Rothiemurchus until the 18th century. Their tartan may be a variant of an earlier Black Watch tartan.

Sinclair

The first Scots to use this name were probably Norman-French supporters of the 12th century Scottish kings. They settled in Lothian with a principal residence at Roslin, but through marriage moved into the Viking earldom of Orkney and Caithness. One line of the family possessed great estates in Caithness and a principal castle in the now ruinous Girnigoe overlooking Sinclair's Bay north of Wick. The Sinclair tartan gives the impression of being a red tartan but is in reality one of the green and blue setts with broad red bands superimposed.

Stewart

The Stewarts have been both kings and clansfolk. They are descended from Norman followers of the 12th-century kings of Scots and, as stewards of the Royal Household, inherited the throne of Scotland through marriage to the daughter of King Robert the Bruce. Stewart families, all claiming royal descent, settled in Atholl in Perthshire and Appin in Argyll. Their tartan may be an early one since shades of red were popular in Gaelic society. The design now known as Royal Stewart has been carefully maintained for at least 200 years. Typical of the product differentiation of 19th-century tartan design is the so-called Dress Stewart in which the broad band of red has been changed to white. A dark tartan now called Hunting Stewart has been popular as a sett worn by those who feel that they may have no claim to a tartan.

Stewart of Appin
A branch of the family of medieval Royal stewards obtained lands in Lorn at the beginning of the 15th century and became a Gaelic clan. One of their chieftains was appointed Chamberlain of the Isles by James IV and he built Castle Stalker on the 'Cormorant's Rock' in Loch Linnie. Their slogan, *Creag an Sgairbh*, commemorates this. Their tartan appears to have been designed in the early 19th century.

Sutherland
The clan originated in the north of Scotland in the area which took its name from the Norse word meaning 'southland'. The creation of an earldom of Sutherland in the early 13th century was designed to create a buffer state between the Norse earldom of the Northern Isles and the kings of Scots. The traditional name of the earls and chieftains of Sutherland has always been *Morair Chat*, 'the lord of cats', and of their territory, *Cataibh*, 'the province of cats'. Their tartan is more or less identical with the Black Watch.

Urquhart
The family and clan takes its name from the district lying on the north shore of Loch Ness where the great castle of Urquhart stands strategic guard between East and West. Their tartan is derived from the Black Watch with the addition of a red stripe and with the black lines moved.

Further reading

Acknowledgements

Carmichael, Alexander. *Carmina Gadelica. Hymns and Incantations ... Orally Collected in the Highlands and Islands of Scotland.* 6 volumes, Edinburgh, 1928-1971.

Dunbar, J T. *The History of Highland Dress.* Edinburgh: Oliver and Boyd, 1962, 2nd edition 1979.

Dwelly, Edward. *The Illustrated Gaelic-English Dictionary.* Glasgow: Alex MacLaren & Sons, 1949 (5th edition), Glasgow: Gairm Publications, 1988 (10th edition).

Grant, I F. *Highland Folk Ways.* London: Routledge and Kegan Paul, 1961, Paperback Editions, 1980.

Grant, I F and Hugh Cheape. *Periods in Highland History.* London: Shepheard Walwyn, 1987.

Hesketh, Christian. *Tartans.* London: Weidenfeld and Nicolson, 1961.

Mackay, J G. *The Romantic Story of the Highland Garb and the Tartan.* Stirling: Mackay, 1924.

McClintock, H F. *Old Irish and Highland Dress.* Dundalk: Tempest, 1943.

MacLean, Calum. *The Highlands.* London: B T Batsford, 1959, Inverness: Club Leabhar, 1975, Edinburgh: Mainstream Publishing, 1990.

Martin, Martin. *A Description of the Western Islands of Scotland, 1703.* Donald J MacLeod (ed), Stirling, 1934.

Munro, R W. *Highland Clans and Tartans.* London: Octopus, 1977.

Scarlett, James D. *Tartans of Scotland.* London: Lutterworth Press, 1972.

Scarlett, James D. *Tartan: The Highland Textile.* London: Shepheard Walwyn, 1990.

Stewart, Donald C. *The Setts of the Scottish Tartans.* Edinburgh: Oliver and Boyd, 1950, revised edition 1974.

Stewart, Donald C and J Charles Thompson. *Scotland's Forged Tartans.* Edinburgh: Paul Harris, 1980.

Stewart, D W. *Old and Rare Scottish Tartans.* Edinburgh: George P Johnston, 1893.

Stewart of Garth, Maj. Gen. David. *Sketches of the Present State of the Highlanders of Scotland.* 2 volumes, Edinburgh: Constable, 1822.

Sutton, Ann and Richard Carr. *Tartans. Their Art and History.* London: Belew Publishing, 1984.

I would like to thank the following for their help in the preparation of this book: James Scarlett, Jack Dalgety, John MacInnes, Angus Fairrie, Harry Lindley, Tom Massey Lynch, Peter MacDonald, Fiona Marwick, Elizabeth Arthur, Charles Burnett, Allan Carswell, George Dalgleish, Cindy Sirko, Richard Martin, Harold Koda, Laura Sinderbrand, Alison Cromarty, and most especially my colleagues Jenni Calder and Pat Macdonald for their essential editorial help; also the Scottish Tartans Museum, Comrie, Aberdeen Museums and Art Gallery, the National Galleries of Scotland, the Scottish National Portrait Gallery, and the National Trust for Scotland for their ready co-operation with the assembling of illustrations.   HC

The following abbreviations are used in attributing illustrations:

NMS	National Museums of Scotland
SEA	Scottish Ethnological Archive, National Museums of Scotland
NGS	National Gallery of Scotland
SNPG	Scottish National Portrait Gallery
AAGM	Aberdeen City Arts Department, Art Gallery and Museums
GMAG	Glasgow Museums and Art Galleries